Persuasive Marketing:

The use of NLP
in Marketing & Advertising

James Brackin & Glyn Parry

Before we start...

...you should be aware that Persuasive Marketing – the use of NLP in Marketing & Advertising is built on two well-founded principles:

1. Like every other animal, humans have built-in fixed action patterns* - these patterns produce predictable responses that are triggered by specific stimuli. Think of these fixed action patterns as instinctive hard-wired shortcuts, originally part of our Freeze, Fight or Flight response, that help us make decisions, behave or act more efficiently. In effect they prompt us to behave in predetermined ways in specific situations.

2. Like every other animal, humans use fixed action patterns to guide our interactions with the world around us. This means that from a psychology perspective we tend to react to marketing and advertising messages in the same way that we react to communication in one-to-one situations. That's because we process them in the same way. We use the same hard-wired fixed action patterns, the same neural pathways, to process all forms of communication and derive their meaning.

In reality our response to advertising does tend to be less immediate or intense than our response to interpersonal one-to-one interactions. This is mainly due to the more remote nature of the medium used. The medium is why we see cold phone calls as more intrusive than cold direct mail or the reason why TV is more persuasive than press advertising – it's not necessarily the message.

The important thing to remember is that the way we mentally process messages from all of those media is the same.

For example, if you ask someone to do something (and the vast majority of marketing and advertising does) you will increase the probability of a successful positive outcome by 42%* if you link your request to a reason. Even if that reason makes little sense or is unrelated to the request it does not reduce the probability of success. For marketing copywriters it has always been a 'golden rule' to link a call to action to a feature or benefit. Experienced copywriters have discovered that it works, which is why they use and will continue to use this fixed action pattern.

But why exactly does it work? Let's use an example. Imagine that you are in a queue to see a movie. You decide you can't wait, go to the front of the queue and say to the person standing there:

"I need to get to the front, would you mind if I push in?"

Studies show that the probability of a successful outcome is around 60%. But if you said:

"I need to get to the front, would you mind if I push in as I'm meeting a friend?"

The probability rises to 94%.

However if you had said:

"I need to get to the front, would you mind if I push in because it's nearly 6.30?"

the probability of success only falls to 93%. And yes, the fact it's nearly 6.30 makes no sense at all and is not relevant to the request in any obvious way.

The conclusion is that the form of reason tagged onto the end of the request has no influence in the probability of success. Now, that's a useful thing to know in order to predict how 'persuasive' marketing copy might be.

What is it that makes the copy, irrespective of its content, predictable? It's the construction, as are many linguistic fixed action patterns. Linguistically the construction of the last two requests are exactly the same, they link an action to a reason or benefit. This linguistic construction is known as a 'complex equivalent' fixed action language pattern. If you are aware of the construction "x because y" it can be used for anything and will always increase the likelihood of a favourable response.

Persuasive Marketing explores these copy based fixed action patterns, specifically in the context of marketing and advertising so that they can be used with objectivity, structure and volition.

To do this an understanding of how we use them to interact with others is required.

That's why the first section of this book will explore concepts well known in Neuro Linguistic Programming (NLP); rapport, communication and body-language, these core fixed action patterns provide a frame of reference that can be used to demonstrate how they are then used in advertising and marketing.

The scientific evaluation of marketing and advertising is nothing new. Benchmarketing® for example, combines NLP, psychometrics, behavioural psychology, forensic linguistics and iconography in order to predict levels of engagement, persuasion and motivation. This is done by identifying the motivations and obstacles of an audience that are hidden within their everyday language and behaviours. Designed to recognise, categorise and measure the triggers for positive and negative behaviour, it uses these psychological constructs to objectively identify, define and quantify audience motivations and obstacles so that marketing messages can be measured against them.

Behaviour is also affected by the individual's personality preferences which is why the relationship between advertising and psychometric profiles is also covered in this book.

Ground research shows a direct link between the use of fixed action patterns and the probability of advertising to engage, persuade and motivate an audience. Persuasive Marketing will provide an introduction to those patterns and how they are used.

Persuasive marketing is more than just a book

Each of the topics covered in this book is accompanied by a video that provides additional information, examples and perspectives. The URL for each is given at the end of the relevant chapter. In addition, at the end of each chapter of the rapport topics there are NLP style exercises that you can do to try out the techniques discussed.

* 1994 Dr Robert Cialdini, University of California

Contents

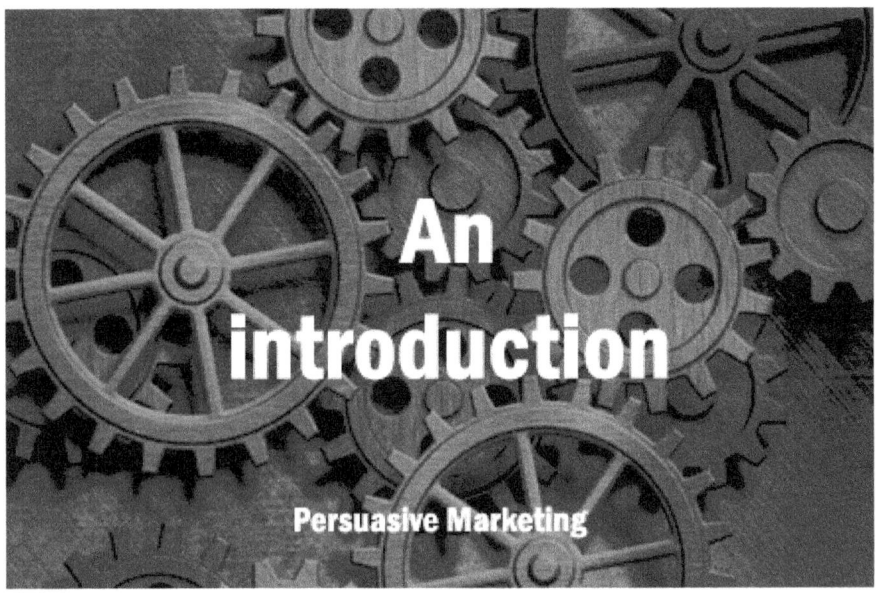

Communication is such a generic term these days; used in many contexts and situations. It covers and describes just about any interaction with others: conversation, teaching, theatre, art, counselling, advertising ….

When you do communicate with another person; you are producing a reaction. And that in turn reacts with your own thoughts and feelings. Your ongoing behaviour is generated by your internal responses to what you see and hear. It is only by paying attention to the other person that you can decide what to say or do next. Your correspondent is responding to your behaviour in the same way.

In direct communication with people, we use words, we use our voice quality, and we use our 'body language': postures, gestures, expressions.

For consistency purposes, we will refer to these as Content, Tone of Voice and Body Language.

Your tone of voice and body language have a massive influence over what we communicate, outweighing the actual content in terms of expressiveness.

For example, a very familiar form of communication in a work environment is the presentation to a group. Research shows that the impact of the communication is determined:

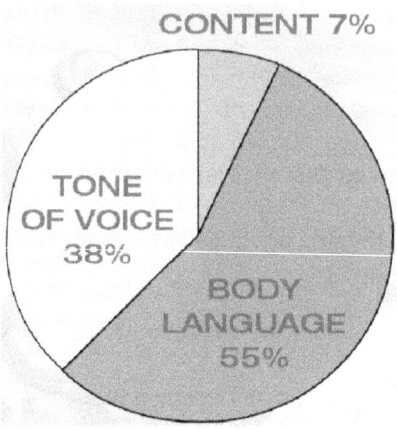

The Journal of Counselling Psychology Vol. 31, 1967, pp.248-52.

55% by the presenter's physiology -

posture, gestures and eye contact

38% by the tone of voice

7% by the content of the presentation

The exact figures will differ in different situations, but clearly body language and tone of voice make an enormous difference to the impact and meaning of what we say.

It's not what we say, but how we say it that makes the difference.

Some politicians spend a great deal of time and effort working on their voice tonality. Try this for yourself; pick any innocuous word or phrase, the word 'Hello' for instance. Tone of voice and body language can determine whether it is received as:

a simple recognition

a threat

a put-down

an enthusiastic greeting

Same content – different communication.

Actors do not really work with words; they are trained in tone of voice and body language and need to be able to convey at least a dozen different shades of meaning with any word, even one as basic as "no".

All of us express many shades of meaning in our everyday conversations and probably have many different ways to say "no", the only difference is we do not consciously think about them, we do it unconsciously.

To think of this as nothing more than the tools for inappropriate manipulation or misrepresentation is to underestimate the scope and significance of these communication characteristics. Communication is a loop anyway, whatever you do influences the other person, and what they do influences you; it cannot be otherwise.

As you already influence others, the only choice is whether to be conscious (aware) or unconscious (unaware) of the effects you create. One of the most natural and powerful ways to influence the effectiveness of your communications is to understand and utilise Rapport.

Rapport

Rapport works on the principal that when people are like each other, they tend to be more responsive. In effect, Rapport allows us to communicate and bond with our audience's unconscious mind. It isn't about pretending to be someone we're not; it is simply an example of appreciating another person's model of the world and adjusting so that we are in tune and better able to communicate together.

When we think about Rapport, assuming we think about it at all, it is usually in the context of direct, face to face interaction. Of course, our indirect interactions such as advertising, direct mail, online – all marketing in fact, also have a physiology, tonality and content, and the audience use the same neurology to unconsciously assess whether there is rapport between us. Because gaining rapport between your marketing and your audience means more engagement, more awareness, more consideration and more response; this is a massively important topic and we will return to it later.

In direct, face to face situations; education, therapy, counselling, business; rapport is essential to establish an atmosphere of trust and participation within which people can respond. And we do this naturally all the time.

So how can we refine and extend this natural skill? And what is it we actually do to gain rapport with people? To get a practical, rather than a theoretical answer, we can turn the question around. How do you know when two people are in rapport? As you look around in restaurants, offices, any place where people meet and talk, can you identify which people have rapport and which do not? Try it for yourself; look for the indicators of rapport. Communication seems to flow when two people are in rapport; their bodies as well as their words match each other.

Our words, our Content, can certainly create or destroy rapport, but as it is only 7% of the communication, the Body Language and Tone of Voice are more significant.

"Monkey see, monkey do"

You may have noticed that people who are in rapport tend to 'mirror' and 'match' each other in posture, gesture and eye contact; they respond and mirror each other's movements with movements of their own. They are engaged in a dance of mutual responsiveness.

Have you ever found yourself enjoying a conversation with somebody and then noticed that both your bodies have adopted the same posture? The deeper your rapport, the closer the match will tend to be. This skill would seem to be inborn, for new-born babies move in rhythm with the voices of the people around them. When people are not in rapport their bodies reflect it - whatever they are saying, their bodies will not be matching. They are not engaged in the dance and you can see it immediately.

Successful people create rapport, and rapport creates trust. You can create rapport with whoever you wish by consciously refining the natural rapport skills that you use every day. By matching and mirroring body language and tonality you can very quickly gain rapport with almost anyone. Eye contact is an obvious area of rapport skill.

Interestingly, it is the only one that is consciously referenced in Anglo-Saxon culture, which has a strong taboo against noticing body language consciously, and responding to it.

However, in this culture, there is usually an assumption that the correct physiology is high levels of sustained eye contact.

Clearly, if we are interacting with someone uncomfortable with eye contact, for whatever reason, that behaviour could cause considerable discomfort and lack of rapport.

To create rapport, join the other person's dance by matching their body language sensitively and with respect. This builds a bridge between you and their model of the world. Matching is not mimicry, which is a noticeable, exaggerated and indiscriminate copying of another person's movements, and is usually considered offensive.

You can match distribution of the body weight, and basic posture. You can match arm movements by small hand movements, body movements by your head movements. This is called 'cross over' matching/mirroring; using some analogous behaviour rather than directly matching. You probably wouldn't match a person's fidgety movements but you could subtly mirror them by swaying your body or with small movements of your hand.

Matching breathing is another very powerful way of gaining rapport. You may already have observed that when two people are in deep rapport they breathe in unison.

These are the basic elements of rapport.

Notice how you feel when you match. Mostly it will feel good to be in a state of clear communication with another person. In some cases you may well feel uncomfortable. And there are some behaviours that you will not want to match directly.

That's okay.

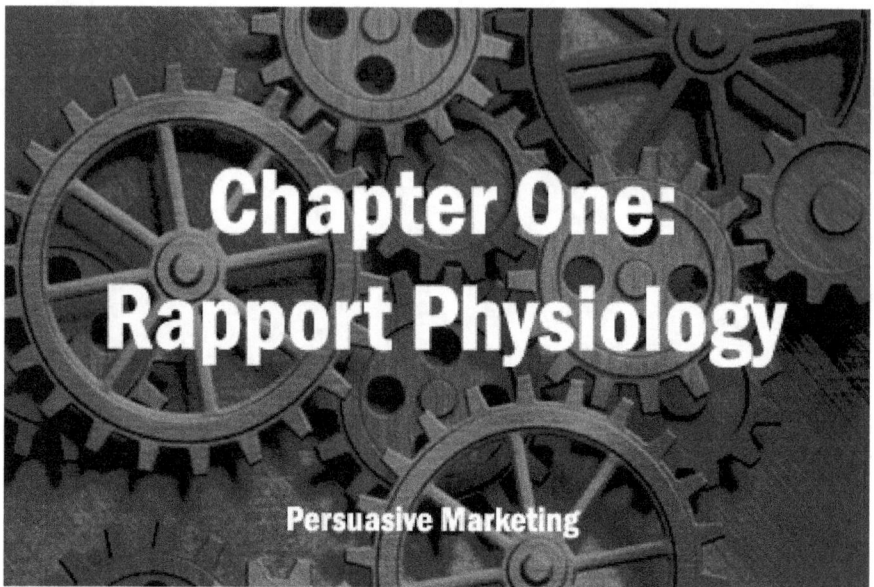

Physiology, often referred to in face-to-face rapport as Body Language, describes any non-verbal communication through the use of postures, gestures, and expressions. You may already be aware that people who are in rapport tend to take up similar postures. The physiology element of Rapport could be described as a dance, where the participants respond and match the other's movements with similar movements of their own.

Have you ever found yourself enjoying a conversation with somebody and noticing that you have adopted a similar posture?

Sometimes the desire for rapport is so strong that one person can trigger a response from thousands. This desire to match body posture is a highly developed skill that all highly social animals possess. Its purpose is to create a bond, a sense of unity and trust.

Pacing physiology to gain rapport.

Physiology, when you have the opportunity, is usually the most effective method to gain rapport. In neuro-linguistic programming (NLP) when you adopt the posture of another, sit or stand in a similar fashion to their physiology, this is called pacing. Pacing is establishing the connection through rapport and respect.

To gain more rapport using physiology there are two basic choices, you can either match or mirror the other person's body language. Both are equally effective, so choose the one that you are most comfortable with.

Mirroring reflects the other person's movement, as if they were looking in a mirror. So, as an illustration, to mirror a person raising their left hand, you would raise your right hand. So why don't you do it right now? Remember I said this might feel a little strange, but that will soon pass.

Now to match the same person who has raised their left hand, you would raise your left hand. Matching is doing exactly the same thing as the other person.

There are just three things you'll want to remember for successful matching and mirroring.

Match or mirror as few elements as possible to gain rapport, the more elements you match the more obvious it is likely to be.

Use small, subtle changes, which don't have to be exactly the same, after all this is rapport, not mimicry. Wait a few seconds before moving, or until you are speaking if matching or mirroring a gesture.

So having the basics, what exactly should we be matching and mirroring. Well the best starting point is posture. Practice it and become comfortable with it before moving on to more specialised or distinctive gestures. Posture provides the broad canvas to which elements can be added. It provides good levels of rapport and is easy to do.

The elements to be aware of and look out for include:

Body Position - Are they sitting, standing, kneeling, slouching?

Body State - Are they relaxed or tense?

Body Angle - Are they leaning in any particular direction?

Limb Position - Are their legs or arms crossed?

Hand Position - Are their hands in their pockets or holding an object?

Head Position - Is their head tilted in a certain direction?

Foot Position - Are their feet together or apart?

Most people punctuate or add emphasis with the use of gestures. Often these are individual in their style and they are more commonly used whilst speaking. The rule with gestures is only to use them in the same context as they were used. For example, if someone makes hand gestures to help illustrate an explanation, you would wait until you were making an explanation before making similar gestures.

Things to look out for when recognising gestures are:

Do they gesture with their hands in a particular way?

Do they gesture with nods of the head or another body part?

Are the gestures large/small/exaggerated/restricted?

Are their gestures toward a particular person or thing?

Do they use gestures to assist in describing objects or

locations?

And finally let's talk about eye contact. Making eye contact is an obvious rapport skill and often the only one that is consciously taught in English culture. The simple rule with eye contact is to match the other person's preference, if they use little or no eye contact then so should you. If they use a lot of eye contact then do the same. If maintaining eye contact makes you feel uncomfortable then here's a tip.

Look at the bridge of the nose, just below the point where the eyebrows would meet. It has exactly the same effect and is much easier to maintain.

You can check your communication to see if you are actually in rapport by "leading." Once rapport has been established most people will attempt to stay in rapport. Leading is the way that you direct the rapport in order to share your ideas and thoughts in a way that they are most likely to be well received. So for example, if you are both sitting with un-crossed legs, you cross your legs, you are subtly changing the rapport. The other person will instinctively wish to maintain rapport and will follow suit and change their physiology. That is assuming you are in rapport, if they do not, then that is a sign that you need to develop more rapport before you communicate your ideas and thoughts.

Rapport allows you to build a bridge to the other person: you have some point of understanding and contact. With that established, you can start to change your behaviour and they are likely to follow. You can lead them in another direction. The best teachers are those who establish rapport, and enter into the world of the learner, and so make it easier for the learner to enter into a greater understanding of their subject or skill. They get on well with their students, and the good relationship makes the task easier.

Leading is changing your behaviour so the other person follows. Leading will not work without rapport. You cannot lead someone over a bridge without building it first.

Core Pattern Physiology

Ideally the meaning given to any posture or gesture should be based on observation of the person within the context of the situation. Just because someone has their arms folded across their body doesn't mean that they are being defensive. It might just be a habit, they might be cold; there are a number of possibilities. Generalisations of this type can give false impressions and should not be relied upon.

That said there are a number of core patterns that can provide a useful guide to anyone who is developing an understanding of the physiology of rapport. There are three basic patterns that can be useful for quickly assessing the state of mind and intention of another person.

An example of a closed body posture

Closed Patterns

The closed pattern is a collection of body postures that are usually associated with defending, hiding, refusing and denying. Closing is a classic defensive move, making the body less vulnerable to attack, and is typically seen when a person feels threatened or anxious in some way.

These moves can also indicate disagreement or dislike, withdrawing the body shows that they are not open or perhaps comfortable with rapport at that time. Closing moves the body into a position which inhibits body movement. In the dance of rapport, it can thus be a sign for you to give something or back off for a while.

The closed pattern can be recognised if the other person:

1. Lowers their head, with chin down – specifically protecting the neck.

2. Closes their mouth and eyes, lowering eyebrows refusing or hesitating to speak or make eye contact.

3. Assumes a defensive posture by crossing their arms or legs, pulling in shoulders, elbows or knees as if protecting their organs and vulnerable parts.

4. Hunching down, or attempting to make the body look smaller.

An example of an open body posture.

Watch the Rapport Physiology video at
http://www.espconsultancy.co.uk/rapport_physiology

Open Patterns

Not surprisingly, these are the opposite of closed patterns and indicate openness, removing barriers and receptiveness. Open patterns are a signal of readiness to listen and accept others. In particular the transition of going from closed to open shows a change of heart, moving away from suspicion and anxiety towards comfort and acceptance which suggests trust.

Signs of openness include:

1. Raising the head from a chin-down position to looking forwards.

2. Unfolding arms, uncrossing legs, increased eye contact.

3. Opening up the body by moving limbs to the sides, increasing height or making the body look larger

Breathing

A subtle way to match physiology, matching breathing will give a deep level of rapport very quickly. The best way to watch how the other person is breathing is to stand slightly to one side (45 degree angle) focus on their face and be aware of how their chest is moving.

With a little practice you will be able to detect their breathing style. To make it easier there are only three options:

1. If the shoulders and the top of the chest move when breathing then they will have fast, shallow breathing which typically is a sign of someone who is in a high tempo, active state.

2. If it's hard to detect any movement then it's likely that they are breathing from the middle of the chest. This is the normal state for most people and suggests someone who is at ease.

3. If you notice the abdomen moving when they breathe than they are breathing from the belly. This is produces deep relaxed breathing, and is a sign of someone who may be very kinaesthetic (see Thinker Feeler personality styles),

Should you choose to match their breathing pattern you will very quickly start to feel the same way as the other person.

Breathing is a powerful mode to build rapport as you will naturally be in 'sync' with their state and you will naturally gain rapport.

Physiology Rapport Exercise

Now try it for yourself. Notice what happens when you match or mirror others. Notice what happens when you stop. Notice what people do who are in rapport.

Start to be conscious of what you do naturally so you can refine it and choose when to do it. The next time you are in conversation with someone notice and match/mirror their:

Posture

Limb positions

Head angle

Gestures

Eye contact frequency and duration

Remember, you can be subtle (cross over) or you can experiment making it more and more overt. Chances are, if you are already in rapport with someone they won't even notice. Now develop your rapport even further, notice and match/mirror their:

Breathing

Pace of speaking

Timbre

Volume

Phrasing and rhythm

Remember, you are not mimicking them, so do not try and copy an accent! It's about getting in tune with their manner of speaking.

Test this out.

If you have the opportunity, try this when you are discussing something you can both agree on. Feel how close and in harmony you both are.

Test this out.

When you are in rapport, change one aspect of your physiology and see if your companion follows you. If they do, they are unconsciously acting to maintain the rapport you are both enjoying. If they don't; it's okay. Go back and try something else.

Test this out.

When rapport is heightened, switch the topic of conversation to something you can both disagree on. Notice how difficult it is to disagree while you are in rapport.

You may find areas of consensus you hadn't considered before, you will certainly respect each other's right to a different view and discuss it constructively looking for common ground.

In extreme cases, if a topic is introduced that is a known area of major contention you may see recalled discomfort represented instantly in a physiological change. Match or mirror to 'hang in there', maintain rapport and gradually bring them back.

Test this out.

Notice what happens when you mismatch.

Mismatching is a very useful skill. The most elegant way to end a conversation is to disengage from the dance. Radically change your physiology, your tone, your volume. The most extreme mismatch of course is to turn your back.

Use this three step process to increase your skill of matching and mirroring physiology

Step One

Become aware of physiology in a safe environment, for example watching people on television, chat shows & interviews are perfect for this. It's an easy non-threatening way to become more comfortable with recognising matching and mirroring as you remotely observe their movements.

Step Two

In a one-to-one situation, choose an appropriate time to practice matching or mirroring just one element of someone else's physiology. Be aware of any changes in the level of rapport.

Step Three

Steadily increase the range and number of elements, you match or mirror at any one time to a maximum of three. Choose the elements that you feel most comfortable with or that are appropriate for the situation and notice the effect they have.

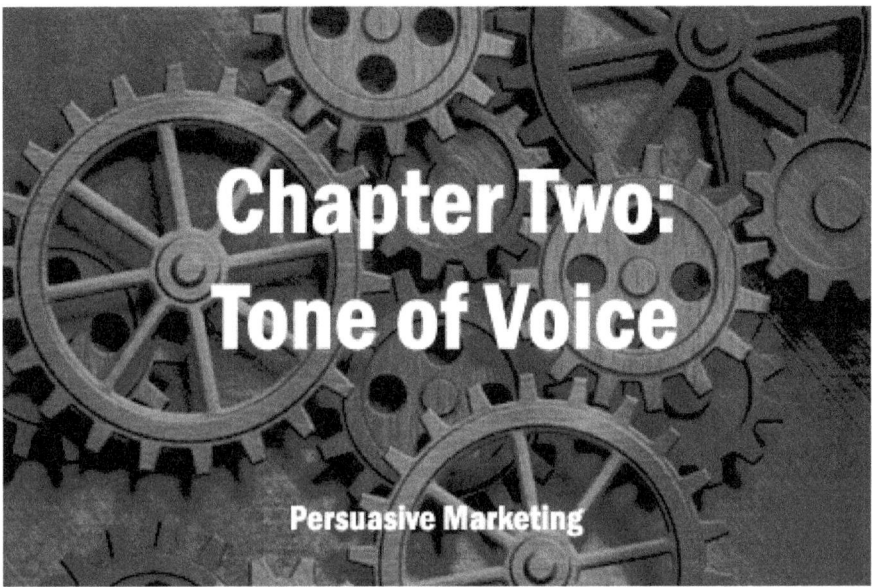

Tone of Voice has a powerful influence on the nature of communication. For example, a very familiar form of communication in a work environment is the presentation to a group. Research has verified that Tone of Voice can exert considerable influence even in a face-to-face communication.

Remember the impact of the communication:

55% by the presenter's physiology - posture, gestures and eye contact

38% by the tone of voice

7% by the content of the presentation

(Mehrabian and Ferris, Inference of Attitudes from Nonverbal Communication in Two Channels' in The Journal of Counselling Psychology Vol. 31, 1967, pp.248-52.)

The exact figures will differ in different situations, but clearly physiology and tonality make an enormous difference to the impact and meaning of what we say.

Tone of voice provides inflection, nuance and meaning for the information being conveyed. We instinctively overlay tone of voice onto the content to influence judgements on credibility, sincerity, importance.

Tone of voice can even have a powerful effect on the meaning of a word because it sets the context for the content. Indeed, our voice tonality and physiology have a massive influence over what we communicate, outweighing the actual content in terms of expressiveness.

It's not what we say, but how we say it that makes the difference.

When you were a child, and you had been outside playing, recall how your mother called your name. You always knew if you were in trouble, or if she was particularly happy to see you return.

Some politicians spend a great deal of time and effort working on their voice tonality. In a related field, actors do not really work with words; they are trained in tonality and physiology and need to be able to convey at least a dozen different shades of meaning with any word, even one as basic as "no".

Try this for yourself; pick any innocuous word or phrase, the word 'Hello' for instance. Test for yourself how the tonality can determine whether it is received as:

a simple recognition

a threat

a put-down

an enthusiastic greeting

The same word delivered in four different ways that instinctively convey four different meanings.

In this instance the word used contributes very little to the communication. All of the rapport or lack of it is derived from the tone of voice.

Same content – different communication.

All of us express many shades of meaning in our everyday conversations and probably have many different ways to say "no" or "hello", the only difference is we do not consciously think about them, we do it unconsciously.

With tone of voice the same word can be made to mean very different things.

You have probably experienced this before. How often has someone said to you or to someone else "I heard what you said but I know what you meant".

Meaning and intention is almost always taken from the Tone of Voice rather than the content which is why it has the potential to be up to five times more influential than the content.

The Phone

Sometimes it's simply not possible to use physiology to gain rapport, on the phone for example. Although it should be noted that even then your physiology will affect the tone of voice. That's why telephone sales people are trained to sit up straight and smile before starting a call because the listener can detect the caller's state.

In addition, there are a number of things that we can do with our voice in order to gain rapport. An important rule for using voice to gain rapport is:

avoid copying accents - You don't have to speak exactly like someone in order to gain rapport.

The things that have most effect on tone of voice, and the things you should become most aware of are:

Breathing – this affects the quality and emphasis of the voice.

Speed or Pace of speaking

Pitch – at the high end or the low end of the speaker's register

Volume – loud or soft

Phrasing and rhythm

When using tone of voice to gain rapport, pick just one element and subtly adjust your voice to be closer to the other person. Remember the purpose is not to match them exactly, just to move closer to their comfort zone.

A deep male voice mimicking a high pitched female voice would be ridiculous, but a female for example, could use the lowest part of her natural register when speaking with a particularly deep voiced male and vice versa.

If someone is agitated, slightly raising the speed and volume of your voice would give them a greater sense of rapport than if you really slowed your voice down and quietly told them to relax. You will usually find that the rapport you create dissipates their negative energy and you can gradually 'lead' them to a more comfortable state.

To practice Tone of Voice, first start to notice the patterns of others. Then when you are confident, perhaps the next time you are on the telephone to someone, slightly adjust your delivery to harmonise with the other person in one of these four aspects:

Speed or Pace

Pitch

Volume

Phrasing and rhythm

One tip is that although you can't see them breathing in this situation, you can notice how they pause. They are almost certainly pausing for breath. Match it and you will be more in tune with their rhythm. Remember, you are not mimicking them, you are harmonising with their manner of speaking.

And conversely, you can use aspects of tone to mark out or emphasise selected parts of what you say, before moving back into rapport. As with all the characteristics we are discussing in Rapport, we do this naturally, unconsciously. So bear in mind how you can choose and determine to do it consciously for particular effect.

Try this little exercise.

Take a sentence and emphasize each word one at a time every time you say the sentence. For example:

I love my job

I **love** my job

I love **my** job

I love my **job**

Notice how the meaning of the sentence changes each time. And of course, as with Physiology, you can use Tone of Voice to deliberately break rapport when you choose to bring a communication to an end.

Next we'll take a look at content which from a marketing communication perspective has a dramatic effect on engagement, memorability and ultimately response.

Watch the Tone of Voice video at
http://www.espconsultancy.co.uk/tone_of_voice

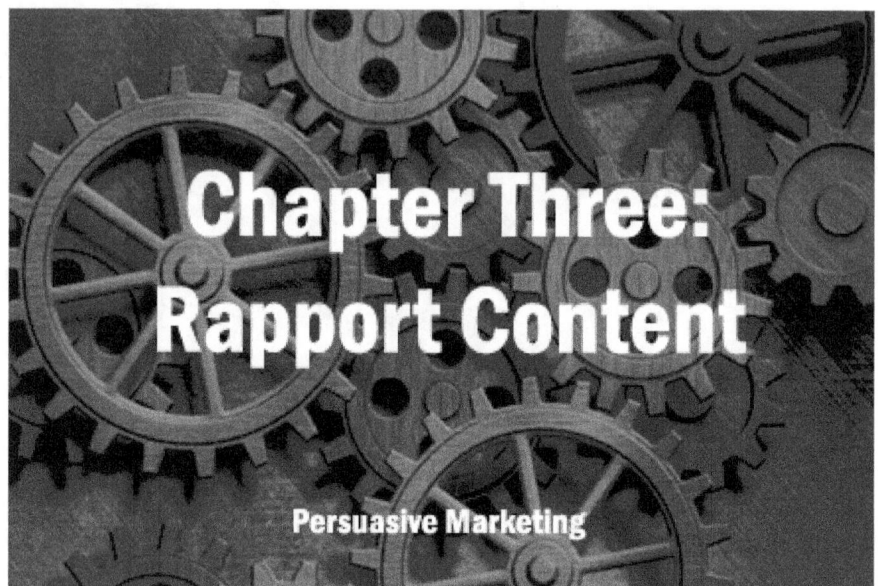

Content: the curse of assumptions

Have you ever had this experience?

You get into a disagreement with somebody about some subject or other, and just when the argument is escalating into something really unpleasant, you realise that this person's perspective on the subject is very different to yours.

Their experience and frames of reference are so different; not necessarily superior or inferior, just different. From your perspective their frames of reference may be peculiar, bizarre and weird; but for sure they are different. Hardly surprising you are disagreeing.

Words, symbols and images are profoundly useful. Imagine a world where we had to invent them anew every day. Life as we know it wouldn't function. But it is easy to forget that they are all just representations and most often representations of incredibly complex entities and concepts.

Symbols have no meaning other than those we give them

What does the CND symbol really represent? Or the Christian Cross? Or the Stars and Stripes? Or your organisation's logo?

What does the swastika represent?

Yes that's right, it's a decorative shape commonly found in Hinduism, Buddhism and Jainism and dating from Neolithic times.

Just think how many very thick books have one or two word titles.

What is 'Life'?

What is 'Death'?

What is 'Justice'?

What happens if you go into an office supplies store in the USA and ask for a box of rubbers?

We all make a natural assumption that everybody thinks about and represents the world in the same way that we do.

As you probably discovered in this module's video segment, we each have different perspectives on commonly used words. In it I asked you to choose seven words that mean the same as 'Quality'. If you haven't already chosen seven, stop reading and do it now.

You had particular meanings for the word 'Quality'. So did I. Mine were:

Reliability

Safe

Expensive

Desirable

Confidence

Guaranteed

You may even have thought that some of my word associations were peculiar, bizarre or weird. And that would be okay, because I might well think the same about some of yours. Either way, if you two needed to debate whether a new piece of your own communication represented 'Quality' in an appropriate manner you would best clarify your frames of reference first.

Once you have a frame of reference it is quite easy to 'match' and 'mirror' the other person's preferred language. For example if you were trying to convince Jim to spend more on a piece of office equipment, knowing his preferences you may say something like:

"This is a quality piece of equipment, it may be more expense but we can be guaranteed that it will be safe and reliable."

Replaying his terms of reference are much more likely to motivate, engage and persuade.

The same is true for marketing communications.

As a result of running that exercise many times, we can confirm that the same experience prevails for any word we have ever tested. Matching and mirroring content gains rapport and is highly responsive. And the same is certainly true of symbols and imagery because in the same way they are associated for us with particular experiences and references.

So, words (like images) are a very useful 'code' that we can all share, but it is vital that we recognise how shallow is any shared or common understanding of meaning.

If that's true, how do we clarify our frames of reference? How do we gain rapport?

In essence, it is the same as physiological and tone of voice rapport. We want to share ideas and thoughts in a way that they are most likely to be well received, so we need to build points of understanding and contact, we need to build that bridge to the other person and enter into their world.

In the same way, that is achieved by matching and mirroring. In this aspect, we are matching and mirroring the content, and in order to do that we must appreciate the other person's frames of reference.

Therefore, the golden rule for gaining rapport using content is not to assume that you know what the other person is talking about or that you understand its meaning. Remember 'the curse of assumptions'; whenever you think you know what someone means, ask yourself in fact you're just assuming they mean whatever you would mean.

You can then use a very simple technique.

You ask a question.

The answer will provide you with more information. And provide it in the form of content that you can replay back to the other person. Often, the simplest way to check your assumptions is to replay the word or phrase to the person using it, with a questioning tone.

For example:

Watch the rapport content video at
http://www.espconsultancy.co.uk/rapport_content

It might not have made a great comedy sketch but if you were the shopkeeper in the video, to avoid confusion and gain clarity, you could have queried;

Forcandles?

To which the reply may well have been "Yeah, handles for forks."

Or you could have asked "When you say Forcandles, how do you mean?"

Either way, asking questions gives you the opportunity to gain rapport by giving the other person the opportunity to talk about their assumptions.

In the example 'Quality', you may find that the other person's reply is still ambiguous or unclear. That's okay, you are gaining rapport and just need elegant ways to ask the same question again; "that's interesting, when you say Quality means it needs to look reliable, how do you know when something like this looks reliable?"

Remember, this is about building a bridge, not an interrogation. Assuming you have the opportunity or can create an appropriate situation, it is an opportunity to show a genuine interest in their perspective and enter into their frames of reference. As such it is a great opportunity to develop rapport. You don't need to agree with the other person's perspective, you certainly don't need to adopt it or make it your own. You just need to appreciate it and 'try it on for size'.

Then it is easier for you to play their words, phrases and terms back to them, safe in the knowledge that you understand them and they will fully understand you.

The same is true when producing marketing communications. A little time spent understanding the frames of reference and language used by your audience to describe your product or service will provide the structure of any content based communication.

We will examine this in much more detail later.

First, we will need to understand another factor that will help you predict how people will respond to communication and guide your choice of layout, tone and content; that is their Personality Traits.

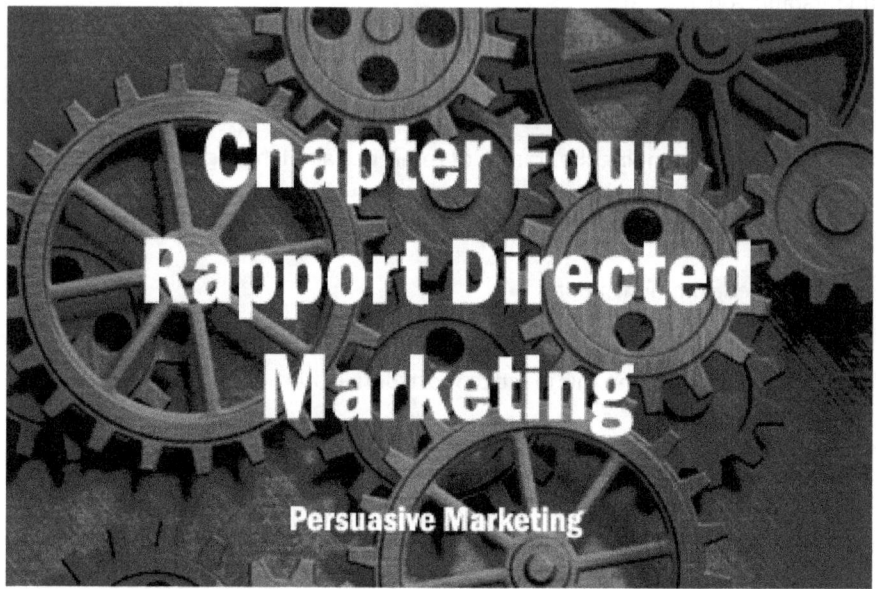

Relating copy and visuals to personality traits

Having an understanding of the basics of rapport and personality types is a useful life-skill in and of itself. But as marketing professionals, eventually we want to know how to apply this to our working environment. That's why the focus of the now turns towards the application of Rapport in a marketing context, using the terminology we have applied in the previous modules.

Now when we are asked to make judgements on something – such as a piece of marketing communication - but not provided with any objective criteria, we all tend to make judgments based on what we like or what we would respond to ourselves. It's very hard to be dispassionate. Objectivity is critically important, because even though the communication execution is largely aesthetic, the primary distinction between marketing and art is a measurable business outcome. Therefore, a robust method for evaluating concepts scientifically is extremely useful.

When we are interested in the effectiveness of communications, understanding the intended audience is of course fundamental. One of the issues with standard research is that it can elicit a variety of interesting things, but it is not designed to scientifically identify and analyse the messaging priorities or persuasion preferences that are intrinsic to gaining the best possible rapport with particular audiences. And it does not provide a direct process for helping communications match those preferences.

Where that matching is achieved, we have optimum rapport with an audience. When we have rapport, the audience is more likely to engage, be motivated and be persuaded by our messages. If you have ever had a campaign that works well with one segment but not at all with another, similar segment, understanding the messaging priorities or persuasion preferences of the two audiences may well tell you why.

And of course, by understanding their preferences and using the techniques in this training, you'll be able to objectively guide the development of marketing materials by assessing their ability to gain rapport with the audience and suggesting ways to enhance that rapport.

Communication Styles and Preferences

Although it may seem obvious, it is not widely understood or appreciated that people with different personality traits tend to be more engaged by different styles and types of communication. In the same way as people instinctively like or dislike people, people instinctively like or dislike advertising. In the same way that people have personality traits, advertising also has personality traits. The only real difference is that people-based personality traits are widely understood, researched and documented, whereas communication personality traits are not.

As a basic rule, our rapport with advertising's visual and linguistic styles is very similar to our rapport with people in a person-to-person situation. Marketing communications can 'match' and 'mirror' personal preferences in order to engage and motivate. And people use exactly the same instinctive processes of Physiology, Tone of Voice and Content to interpret marketing communications as they do person-to-person interactions.

The techniques contained within this training are extrapolated from those basic rapport skills you have experienced in the earlier parts of this training module; transposed into a marketing context. All of the techniques have in direct tests or independent research been proven to have a consistent, positive effect on marketing materials' ability to communicate information that is retained, spontaneously recalled and responded to.*

*Millward Brown 2006

Matching communications to the preferences of your audience is such an important technique because it is possible to take different elements of the communication and evaluate them objectively against defined rapport benchmarks. So this still allows a subjective analysis of communications, but it also provides a consistent framework by which they can be evaluated, debated and developed.

Although most marketing professionals concentrate their efforts on changes to content, just as in person-to-person rapport, that is not always the element with the most potential to influence.

A more robust way to evaluate your marketing communications

Systematic analysis of a communication's 'Body Language' is a complex process that requires the use of Benchmarketing software. However, there is value in recognising and quantifying some of the structures even in a more informal situation. Whilst a full comparative analysis requires the same understanding of the audience for comparison, adopting a structural view of the communications will inevitably highlight interesting points of difference and enable a better quality of debate and appreciation.

In face-to-face rapport, we don't need to interpret people's Physiology or Tone, the issue is matching them. Likewise in marketing communications, the aspects of Physiology and Tone may relate to particular mental states, personality preferences and groups of people, the issue is recognising them and appreciating how they are manifested in different pieces of communication. So we have included some Hints and Tips on what to look for.

With Personality Trait and Content, it is easier to provide a format for analysis of a communication which though it might lack the detail of the software, will give a useful, structural and objective view. Even when applied without the corresponding analysis of the audience's personality or motivational preferences, it does allow some intelligent estimation of those and provides an excellent format for comparing different pieces of communication. So we have included a guide for assessing Personality Trait and Content of communications in this way.

This guide can be used as part of a structured process that will enable you to produce your own communication evaluation. Though the process might be more approximate than a full analysis, it is consistent and can be applied across any media. Because, rather than relying upon a subjective judgement, it systematically deconstructs a communication into its structural elements and checks them against known rapport features, the scores build into a profile which can then be usefully compared with other communications, including those of your competitors.

This guide provides a solid foundation on which you can always overlay your own experience and judgement. It also provides a useful framework for providing constructive feedback to anyone directly involved in the development, creation or production of the communications.

Typically communications with similar profiles will engage, motivate an audience to respond in similar ways. But for greater accuracy match communications against other influencing factors e.g. known response rates and look for trends.

Rapport Hints - Physiology

In Module 1.2's person-to-person communications, we became consciously aware of Physiology or body language so that we could respond to it and choose to match or mirror it for rapport purposes.

In marketing communications, the physiology is often referred to or generalised in terms such as 'style'. As in person- to-person communications, the Physiology of a piece sends very powerful unconscious signals to the viewer. There are three key elements we should be consciously aware of:

Size

The physical size of the communication determines not only its impact but also the personality type that is attracted to it. For example, Extroverts tend to prefer physically larger communications than Introverts.

Visual Copy Ratio (VCR)

The proportions of space or time given either to copy or to visual elements also greatly influence rapport. For example, a high visual ratio is more likely to appeal to a Big Picture- Impulsive personality, whereas a high text ratio will connect more with a Detailed-Planned profile.

Visual Copy Density (VCD)

The density of the visuals and copy within the available space or time will directly relate to a person's unconscious perception of quality, price and urgency. Generally, the lower the VCD the more likely the perception of quality, price and urgency.

Rapport Hints – Tone

Tone of Voice in person-to-person communication is the aspect with the second biggest potential impact. In marketing communications this equates to what we might traditionally refer to as Layout as the way that the content is displayed gives it a framework, a look, a Tone. Interestingly, this one area is the one on which most brand guidelines concentrate. For the purposes of considering rapport or comparing different communications, there are four distinct areas we should consciously be aware of and take note of:

1. Colours

Colour Type

Primary colours tend to be more assertive.

Tertiary colours tend to be more compassionate.

Intensity

Intense colours appeal more to extroverts.

Muted colours appeal more to introverts.

Colour Coverage

High coverage tends to suggest immediacy and low cost.

Low coverage tends to suggest sophistication and quality.

Colour Number

High numbers tend to suggest urgency and need.

Low numbers tend to suggest stability and confidence.

2. Typography

Open: with generous areas of white space or minimal content, minimal type or image styles. This conveys confidence, quality and trustworthiness

Busy: with little white space, a mixture of layout styles, typefaces and image combinations. This conveys a more 'down market', unsophisticated and bargain message.

3. Number of elements

The more elements there are, the more likely it is that the communication will be viewed as less Brand or corporate image focused and more product or practically focused

4. Image sizes and shapes

Either copy or visuals should dominate a communication. The rule of thumb is the 60/40 rule. 60% visuals for brand messages, product launches etc. 60% copy for sales and information messages

Complex shapes can provide impact and interest, but may well distract from the main message. Use sparingly or to change the pace of a communication.

Rapport Guide – Personality Traits

Personality Traits can, as we have already discovered, be expressed and quantified within a defined framework. Ideally, we need to elicit and quantify the audience preferences in order to accurately evaluate a communication.

However, assessing communications against the defined framework does provide a consistent and structured way to compare them with each other or even sense-check them against existing insights into the audience.

So, we have included a Practical Guide to Assessing Personality Traits available at the end of this topic and it is available as a PDF download via www.espconsultancy.co.uk/persuasive_marketing

It is designed to provide an assessment of a piece of communication. Because it's best to go with your first impression, typically this takes between one and three minutes to complete. Simply answer the eight questions and you will be able to predict the type of person the communication will appeal to.

The Guide can be used without any knowledge of rapport or personality traits so please try it before completing the next topic. However, an understanding of personality traits will greatly improve your use of the Guide and therefore its accuracy.

Typically, the guide can be used to provide additional insight in the three most common marketing communication situations:

Improving Communications using the Guide

To replicate a successful campaign

1. Assess the successful communication against the Rapport Hints and the Practical Guide to obtain a 'profile'

2. Identify the most distinguishing elements of the profile (these may be even more apparent if you can also assess an unsuccessful communication to the same audience)

3. Highlight one key element

4. Use this profile to brief for a new communication with a structural match

5. Create new communication

6. Assess against briefing profile (4)

7. Test campaign and measure results

To improve an unsuccessful campaign

1. Assess the unsuccessful communication against the Rapport Hints and the Practical Guide to obtain a 'profile'

2. Identify the most distinguishing elements of the profile

3. Change one key element in two of the three Guide areas

4. Use the new profile to brief new communication

5. Create new communication

6. Assess against unsuccessful communication

profile for desired variances

7. Test campaign and measure results

To target a new, different or distinct audience

1. Make an assessment of the audience profile

using the Practical Guide Personality Traits and

Rapport Hints

2. Construct an audience profile

3. Identify the key elements of the profile

4. Use the new profile to brief new communication

5. Create communication

6. Assess against constructed audience profile

7. Test campaign and measure results

Alternatively

1. If available, assess any successful communication to that audience even for a different product or service or even from another provider

2. Construct a profile

3. Identify the most distinguishing elements of the profile and use to brief the new communication

4. Create new communication

Watch the Rapport Directed Marketing video at

http://www.espconsultancy.co.uk/rapport_directed_marketing

Determine the underlying
personality type of communications

The images show?

More than three people or faces	
One to three people or faces	
Parts of people but no faces	
No people	

allocate a total of 100 points

+ = I E = +

The text is constructed in?

The singular	
I, me, myself, you, your	
The Plural	
We, they, us, them	

allocate a total of 100 points

Are the Visual elements?

Illustrations	
Photographs	
Charts or Graphs	

allocate a total of 100 points

+ = D B = +

The text is?

Specific, Detailed, Factual	
Stories, Concepts, Promises, Ideas	

allocate a total of 100 points

The images show?

People based product benefits	
Product used by people	
Product	
Product Features	

allocate a total of 100 points

+ = T F = +

What type style(s) are used?

Sans Serif, CAPITALS or Block	
Sans Serif - upper and lowercase	
Serif	
Serif italic, informal sans, drawn, distorted, handwriten	

allocate a total of 100 points

The layout is?

Freeform or informal Cut out images, white space, decorative type	
Structured or rigid. Squared up pictures and type	

allocate a total of 100 points

+ = P M = +

Does the message include?

Ordered and structured arguements	
Numbering, bullet points or call ot panels	
Reasons for immediate action	
Time limited or restricted reasons for action	

allocate a total of 100 points

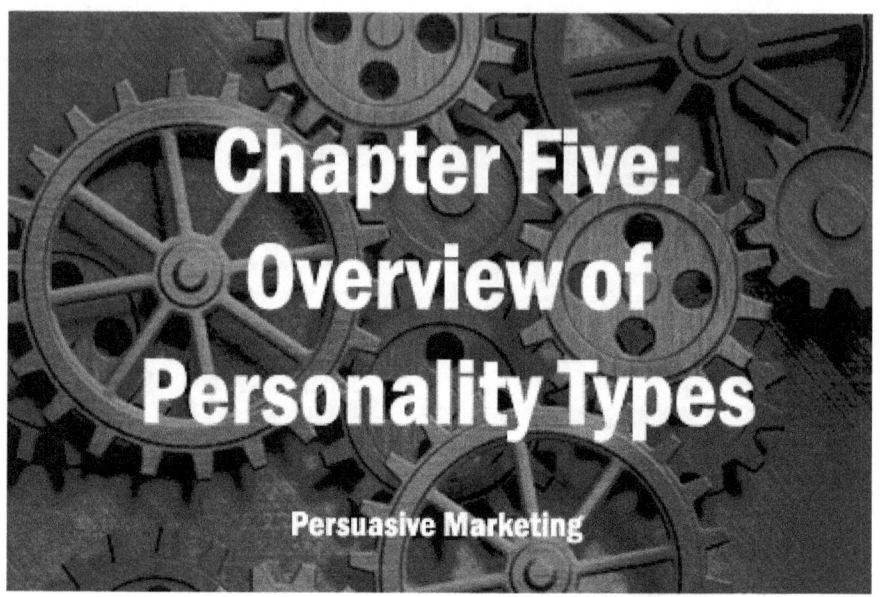

Personality type or trait?

A Distinction.

Personality Typing seeks to classify people into distinct and well-established categories; into this or that type; Introvert or Extrovert, Planned or Impulsive etc.

'Personality Types' refers to categories that are distinct and discontinuous. E.g. you are either one or the other.

The Personality Trait approach identifies particular behaviours as points on a natural 'trait' continuum. To appreciate the difference between types and traits, consider the example of the personality dimension of "introversion".

We can express introversion as:

A Personality Type: you are either an Introvert or an Extravert. This implies that you will (almost) always behave in 'type'.

A Personality Trait: you can be anywhere on a continuum ranging from highly Introvert to highly Extrovert. This means that when predicting behaviour in different contexts, there are naturally occurring degrees of probability by which we will behave 'in' or 'out of type'.

As we will discover later, Personality Traits provide the most efficient predictive models for understanding engagement, motivation and response to direct and indirect communications.

Personality Profiling: Its Origins

What we currently call Personality Profiling can be traced back more than eighty years to the work of C.G. (Carl) Jung, the Swiss-born psychiatrist. In his 1923 book Psychological Types, Jung proposed that human behaviour was not random but was in fact predictable and therefore classifiable.

However, the concept of profiling a person's personality can be found way back in ancient Greece. From Hippocrates in 400 BC through to Galen in 150 AD, Greek philosophers classified people into 4 types. Each type was believed to correspond with an excess of one of four bodily fluids, so the personalities were termed "humours".

Jung differed from many of his counterparts in that his theories not only dismissed the correlation with bodily fluids; they also distinguished between psychological type and the issue of psychological sickness or abnormalities. Jung argued that the differences in our observed behaviour are a natural result of preferences we have for the most basic functions in our personalities; preferences we exercise throughout life. These preferences develop in early childhood, and thus form the foundation of our personalities.

Jung's work remained just a theory for many years. It was World War II and some of the challenges it imposed on the workplace that were the catalyst for the development of a practical and robust psychological profiling instrument. Katharine Briggs had been experimenting with methods of classifying people from early in the 1900's, independent of Jung. Indeed, her observations and distinctions around differences in living styles and approaches to life were already well-formed when Jung's work was published in 1923. At that point however, Briggs became a student of Jung's and throughout the 1930's; with her daughter

Isabel Briggs Myers, she worked on methodologies for classifying people's observable behaviour.

In the early 1940's, the need for so many people to contribute to the war effort inevitably led to many people working in tasks unsuited to their abilities. Myers and Briggs succeeded in designing a psychological instrument that would explain, in scientifically robust and reliable terms, how the differences theorised by Jung could be measured and put to practical use. The Myers-Briggs Type Indicator (MBTI) became the first modern personality profiling instrument, establishing the idea that it was possible to identify individual preferences and then make practical, constructive use of the differing preferences between people.

Today there are many psychological profiling instruments available; all based on the original Jungian model. It is estimated that 85 million people worldwide have been profiled.

Crucially, for anyone interested in the interaction between people and other forms of indirect communications, Jung pointed out how our preferences not only form the core of our attractions and aversions to people, but also to tasks, events and other interactions. Just as we all relate to, pay attention to, trust and remember certain people more than others; we also relate to, pay attention to, trust and remember certain communications more than others.

Eight Basic Types: with infinite variations

The most effective way to understand our 'type' is to take a Personality Trait Indicator.

Whilst there are many Jungian-based indicators available online (Myers-Briggs still being the most well-known) they all use a combination of word-based forced choices. Therefore, even for a subject not experienced in working out how the tests work, they still require 158 separate questions in order to elicit a reliable profile.

However, type indicators that use a combination of word and image-based prompts tend to require fewer questions to provide reliable results because image selection is more 'un-conscious'.

Developed by us, the Greenwich University Personality Trait Indicator (PTI) is such an example and can be found at http://gre.espsurvey.co.uk

The descriptions of the basic traits in this workbook use terminology from the Personality Trait Indicator. They will provide you with a good working framework and enable you to obtain an informal determination of people's preferences.

Use the descriptors below and you will begin to develop an increasing understanding of your own preferences, as well as those of others.

To begin, here is a list of examples to help you translate everyday behaviour in profiling terms. By counting the proportion of statements in each section you agree with, you will see your relative preferences begin to emerge.

As you read the statements below, you will find that you agree with some strongly, some less so, and some not at all.

You may find that while you connect strongly with some of the statements attributed to, say, Extraverts, you will also connect with some of those attributed to Introverts. The same will probably be true for each of the other three pairs of preferences. This is quite normal because we're dealing with personal preferences not fixed types.

Each of us has some Extroversion and some Introversion (as well as some of each of the other six characteristics). The descriptors are not black and white or absolute as each of us has a blend, and it's that blend that reveals our unique personality.

The key to understanding any individual is to determine which alternatives they prefer to use.

As we stated earlier, we'll be looking at four pairs of preference alternatives. There are others, but these are far and away the most significant in understanding communication with most people.

In each case, the distinctions form a continuum and the terms used represent the opposing extremes.

Introversion vs. Extroversion

Ok, so we all know people who are 'party animals' and people who are 'loners'. But fundamentally, this aspect of personality relates to the way we prefer to interact with the world and the way we prefer to receive information, stimulation and energy.

If you are Extrovert (E) you probably recognise and relate to a number of these preferences:

Reading or having a conversation while there is other activity going on (such as another conversation, television or radio) doesn't bother you at all; you can easily ignore that kind of distraction.

You display a tendency to talk first, think later. You don't know what you'll say until you hear yourself say it; often you will chastise yourself; "When will I learn to keep my big mouth shut?"

You know a lot of people and would consider many of them among your close friends; you prefer activities that include as many people as possible.

Friends, colleagues (and strangers) find you approachable. You are easily engaged in interaction and often become dominant in a conversation.

You find telephone calls to be welcome interruptions.

Whenever you have something to say or something occurs to you, you won't hesitate to call or drop-in on someone.

You enjoy meetings because they are an opportunity to express your opinions. Indeed, you would feel frustrated if you were denied the opportunity to put your point of view.

You prefer planning and creating ideas with a group of people rather than doing it alone. If you spend too much time in solitary, reflective thinking where you can't bounce ideas off other people you find it tiring and unfulfilling.

Listening is more difficult than talking; it's boring when you can't participate actively or set the direction of a conversation.

You 'think aloud', verbalise and share your situation; if you have mislaid something you may say (to no-one in particular): *"where have I put my keys? They must be here somewhere"*.

When you need to recapture a train of thought you will verbally 'find' your way back: *"Now, where was I? Oh, yes, I know what it was"*.

Affirmation from colleagues both senior and junior is important and necessary for you. You may think you are fine, looking all right and doing a good job, but in order to know for sure it's good to hear it from others.

If you are Introvert (I) you probably recognise and relate to a number of these preferences:

You rehearse and try out things before speaking and often wish that others would do the same; when asked for an opinion you often reply *"I'll have to think about that"* or stall with *"Um, that's interesting ....."*

You like peace and quiet and enjoy having time to yourself; you dislike having your private time and thoughts invaded by others; you have to protect yourself if you can by developing powers of concentration that exclude radios, telephones and other external distractions.

Other people tell you you're a 'great listener'; to such an extent you are often concerned that they are taking advantage of you.

People sometimes refer to you as "shy"; whether you agree that you are or not, you may come across to others as reserved and reflective.

You like to share special occasions with just one other person or perhaps a few close friends.

Sometimes you wish that you could project your ideas and opinions more forcefully; and you find it annoying when others just blurt out what you were about to say.

You should be able to present your thoughts or feelings without being interrupted; you allow others to do that and expect them to reciprocate when it is your time to speak.

If you've spent time in meetings, on the phone, or socialising with people you need to 'recharge your batteries' alone or with one significant other; the more intense the interaction with people, the more likely you are to feel drained.

As a child, if your parents ever told you to *"go outside and play"* they probably worried that you preferred to be by yourself rather than in a group of friends.

You are suspicious of people who are too complimentary as you believe that 'talk is cheap'; you are also irritated when people repeat something that's already been said or chatter in a group going over and over the same ground.

Remember that these are preferences. It is likely that you've agreed with a number of statements under each preference.

Some people will agree with every Extroverted statement and none of the Introverted; indicating a strong preference for Extraversion.

Others will agree with half the Extroverted statements and half the Introverted ones; indicating a slight preference for one over the other.

Remember there are no good or bad types; only differences. And that everything is relative; displaying strong, weak or inconsistent preferences is perfectly natural.

Detailed vs. Big Picture

This aspect of personality relates to the way we prefer to gather, manipulate and communicate data

If you are Detailed (D) you probably recognise and relate to a number of these preferences:

You prefer specific answers to specific questions; when you ask someone the time, you prefer "three fifty-two" and find it unsatisfactory if the answer is "just before four" or "almost time to go".

You like to concentrate on what you're doing right now rather than wondering about what's next; overall you would rather do something than think about it.

The jobs you find most satisfying are those that yield some tangible result.

You subscribe to the idea that *"if it ain't broke, don't fix it"*; you don't understand why some people are always trying to change everything.

You would rather work with facts and figures than ideas and theories; you like to hear things sequentially instead of randomly.

Fantasy is a silly waste of time; you have to wonder about people who spend too much time indulging their imagination.

You read magazines and reports from front to back; it is odd the way some people seem to dip in and out of them anywhere they please.

You find it frustrating when people don't give you clear instructions or when someone says, *"Here's the overall plan - we'll take care of the details later"*; or even worse, when you've heard clear instructions and others treat them as vague guidelines.

You are very literal in your use of words and take things literally; you often find yourself asking, and being asked, *"Are you serious or is that a joke?"*

You prefer to focus in on your own job or department and aren't as concerned about how it fits into the larger scheme of things.

If you are Big Picture (B) you probably recognise and relate to a number of these preferences:

You tend to think about several things at once; you are often accused by friends and colleagues of being absentminded.

For you the future and its possibilities are more intriguing than frightening; you are usually more excited about where you're going than where you are.

You prefer it if other people take care of the 'boring details'.

You believe that time is relative, no matter what the hour; you aren't late unless the meeting/meal/event has started without you.

You like identifying how things work just for the pleasure of it.

You like puns and word games.

You are interested in the connections and relationships between most things rather than accepting them at face value; you're always asking, *"What does that mean?"*

You tend to give general answers to questions; you don't understand it when people can't follow your directions or insist on specifics.

You would rather focus on spending in the future rather than balancing your account.

Again, you have probably related to examples in both sets of preferences. Remember, everyone has some Detail characteristics and some Big Picture ones.

Also, it is quite natural to perceive things differently at different times. At some point in the year, even the most Big Picture person must deal with the detail of their income tax return.

As you read these example statements and identify your preferences, you'll probably find some preferences emerging more clearly than others. This, too, is natural.

Thinker vs. Feeler

To stereotype this as a contrast between the clinical, rational and 'left brained' and the fuzzy, emotional and 'right brained' is a gross simplification. This aspect of personality does relate to our preferred ways of making decisions but again it includes many levels of overlap and degrees of preference.

If you are Thinker (T), you probably recognise and relate to a number of these preferences:

You are able to stay cool, calm, and objective in situations when other people are upset.

You prefer to settle a dispute based on what is accurate and truthful rather than on what will make people happy.

You enjoy proving a point for the sake of clarity; it's not unknown for you to argue both sides in a discussion simply to expand the intellectual horizons.

You are more firm-minded than gentle-hearted; if you disagree with people, you would rather tell them than say nothing and let them think they're right.

You pride yourself on your objectivity; some people think you are being cold and uncaring; you know this couldn't be further from the truth.

Sometimes difficult decisions are inevitable and you don't mind making them. You can't understand why so many people get upset about things that aren't relevant to the issue at hand.

You think it's more important to be right than to be liked; you don't believe it is necessary to like people in order to be able to work with them and do a good job.

You are more impressed and convinced by things that are logical and scientific; for example, until you receive more information to justify the claims made for Personality Typing you will be sceptical about what it can do.

You remember numbers and figures more readily than faces and names.

If you are Feeler (F), you probably recognise and relate to a number of these preferences:

You believe that a 'good decision' is one that takes into account the feelings of others.

You feel that 'love" cannot be defined; you are annoyed and offended when people try to do so.

You often stretch yourself in order to meet other people's needs; you are prepared to do almost anything to accommodate others, even at the expense of your own comfort.

You are likely to put yourself into other people's shoes; you are the one who asks, "How will this affect the other people involved? How will they feel? What will they do?"

You enjoy providing services to people although you find that some people take advantage of you.

Sometimes you can't help wondering, *"Doesn't anyone care about what I want?"* although you are unlikely to actually say that to anyone.

You are ready to apologise and take back something you've said if you think it has offended someone unnecessarily; you wonder if other people think you are wishy-washy.

Harmony is more important to you than clarity.

You are uncomfortable when there is conflict and prefer to try and either avoid it or suppress it.

Note: Thinker/Feeler is the only preference dynamic that has a relationship to gender. About 60% of all males are Thinkers, and about the same proportion of females are Feelers. Again, this is neither right nor wrong nor is it a fixed rule; it is only a minor preference.

Also, as you assess your own preferences to each set of these examples you may find it interesting to check your self-perceptions against a friend's or colleague's perception of you. Sometimes other people observe our traits in ways we can't see ourselves.

Planned vs. Impulsive

This final set of preferences relates to how people prefer to orient their lives and events within them; either as structured, sequential and organised or as spontaneous, adaptive and flexible.

If you are Planned (P), you probably recognise and relate to a number of these preferences:

When you arrange to meet someone, you are always waiting for them, as most other people never seem to be on time.

You have a place for everything and you aren't rally satisfied until everything is in its place.

It's frustrating that if everyone would just do what they're supposed to do, when they're supposed to do it, the world would be a better place.

You wake up in the morning and know pretty much what your day is going to be; you have a schedule and you follow it. You dislike it if things don't go as planned.

You do not like surprises.

You keep lists and use them; if you do something extra that wasn't on your list, you may just add it so you can cross it off.

You thrive on order; and have special systems for keeping and organising thing.

Sometimes you are accused of being angry when you're just stating your opinion.

You like to complete things and get them out of the way even if you know you'll have to revisit some of them to get them right.

If you are Impulsive (M), you probably recognise and relate to a number of these preferences:

You are easily distracted; you can get 'diverted' between your desk and the door.

You love to explore things that are new, even if it's something as simple as a new route home from work.

Instead of planning a task, sometimes it's better to wait and see what it needs; people who don't understand accuse you of being disorganised.

You can use last-minute bursts of energy to meet deadlines; whilst others are panicking and fretting, you know you will probably make it.

Although you would prefer to have things in order, you know neatness isn't as important as creativity, spontaneity and responsiveness.

You turn most work into play; if it can't be fun, it probably isn't worth doing.

You often change the subject in conversations as new topics that need to be explored can come to mind at any time.

You like to keep your options open; and don't like to be pinned down about most things.

You tend to make things less than definite from time to time, but not always; it depends.

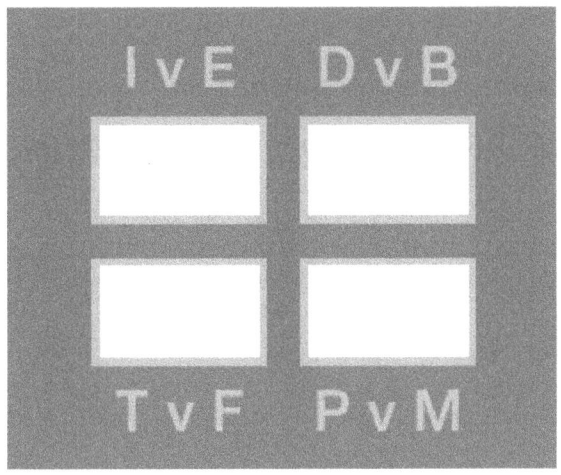

Personality Typing Grid.

Watch the Personality Types video at
http://www.espconsultancy.co.uk/personaility_types

Just for fun … Did you agree with more of the Extroverted statements than the Introverted ones? If so, enter E in the first box above; if you agreed with more Introverted statements, enter I. Then do the same with each of the other three pairs of preferences.

Remember personality traits are not intended to be carved in stone - or even written in ink, so you may like to try a proper Personality Profile. The University of Greenwich Personality Trait Indicator will provide a one page snapshot of your current personality traits and can be found at

http://gre.espsurvey.co.uk

Over time you may find yourself erasing one or more of these letters, because you'll be increasing your knowledge of how each of the eight preferences comes into play in a variety of situations, as well as gaining a fuller understanding of people's preferences - and how to use them to create communications that just seem to 'make sense', 'hit the spot', sound right' and 'look good'.

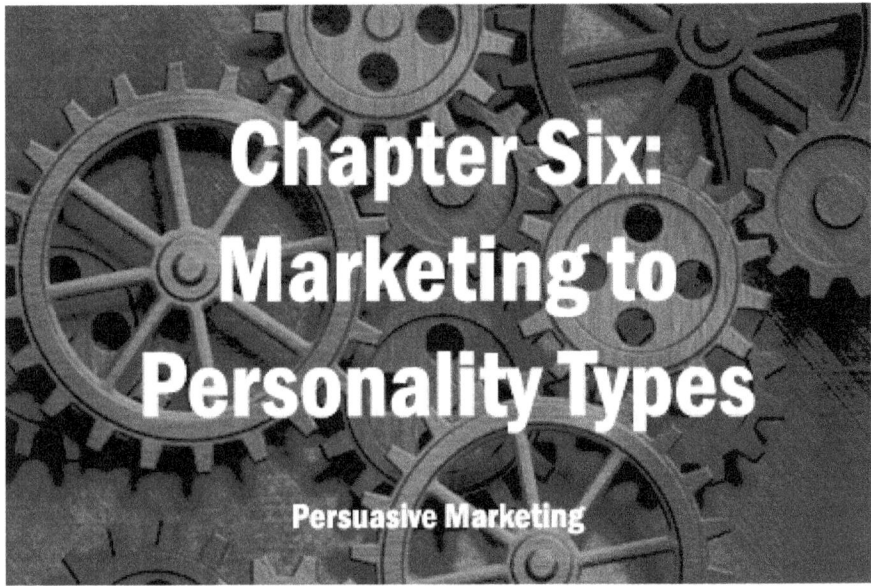

Relating marketing and advertising to personality traits is a fascinating and potentially crucial part of maximising the effectiveness of a communication.

Most of the time we deal with differences between people instinctively, or ineffectually! It is not a factor generally considered when communications are developed or judged, perhaps because in most instances there is no methodology available to deal with it. And yet, you will now appreciate, especially after the last chapter, just how fundamental this is to the way different people relate to interactions.

You will know, considering your own Personality Traits, how a communication that is totally in rapport with you will be so much more engaging and appealing to you than one which is totally the opposite. We might say that getting Personality Traits in a communication spot-on is very, very powerful, getting it partly correct is good but getting it wrong is potentially disastrous.

So, how do we put this to practical use?

First, when we are communicating with individuals

An understanding of an individual's personality traits enables extremely powerful rapport in any communication. Consider for a moment, any time you have communicated with someone who is very Big Picture. And by the way, it is worth noting that the higher one goes in any corporate structure the more likely one is to find a high proportion of Big Picture people.

Just imagine how unwelcome a very detailed explanation of something would be for them. Imagine instead, a top line summary for them with no more than three, key supporting points.

Now, imagine presenting the same top line summary to someone who is very Detailed. If it is on a piece of paper, they will probably turn it over looking for the 'proper' report.

So, this topic is invaluable in guiding interactions with known individuals or small groups of individuals.

Larger groups (audiences) we don't know individually.

Some groupings or clusters will share common personality traits to a high degree. This is particularly true in groups defined by profession or special interest where that profession or interest itself attracts a particular personality trait profile. Eliciting the personality traits from a representative sample would identify any shared profile and enable the tuning of communications to that prevailing profile.

However, with more interactions taking place over computer networks, we are able to engage with very large numbers of individuals and elicit information from them via a Personality Preference Indicator. This enables a record of personality trait (and other useful motivational and rapport characteristics) to be kept and used for automated tuning of any communication to those individuals.

Audiences we don't know individually and can't profile.

Inevitably, we can't always have the advantages of knowing individual personality traits.

We want our press advertising to engage and appeal to as many of the magazine's readers as possible.

We want our presentation to 20 complete strangers to engage and appeal to as many of them as possible.

We want our brochure to engage and appeal to as many of the people it reaches as possible.

In these circumstances, we must assume that our prospect audience is a cross-section of the personality traits continuum we discussed in the last chapter.

Therefore, the issue is; to what extent does the communication deliver across that continuum?

Frequently, when we analyse client communications to a mass audience, we are not helping to tune it to a specific profile, we are revealing an existing focus which might be inappropriate or at least extremely limiting. It can be a sobering moment to realise that a beautifully crafted and extremely expensive creative execution will only really appeal to 32.5% of its prospect audience.

The key learning is not about sacrificing strong ideas in favour of 'something for everybody' or for diluting concepts to the bland. It is an objective guide that asks, is 32.5% okay?

Often small structural changes can dramatically increase the appeal or show what would be required to engage and attract the rest of the prospect audience.

Overall, appreciation of these crucial structures is important because they are so fundamental to your audience's reaction to your communications and yet most people, including many in marketing departments and advertising agencies are often unaware of them.

You will not be surprised to learn that in almost all cases where analysis reveals communications with audience-limiting profiles, the communication is perfectly in rapport with the personality traits of the creative team or the client individual who has most influenced or affected the process. How natural. Those individuals have produced a communication that for them is just perfect. How unconscious. It is just the same as the 'curse of assumptions'. Unless we have an objective guide, our natural assumption is that everyone views and processes the world around us in the same way we do.

So, in summary.

1. Ideally: Identify individuals' Personality preferences whenever you can

2. Or: Identify any cohesive group's Personality profile if possible

3. At the very least: Appreciate the desirability of delivering to as many points on the Personality Traits continuum as possible in any communication or sequence of communications

Above all; understand these personality-based characteristics and be able to apply them to any communication in copy or visual form

How to use this information

If you are using the paper based version of the Personality Guide and have access to your audience profile or other psychometric research.

1. Use the research to make a judgement about/identify the audience profile.

2. Match your communication content to the audience profile.

3. Use the Personality Guide to score the resulting communications, and adjust until a suitable match is obtained.

If you use paper based version of the Personality Guide but you have no psychometric research:

1. Make a valued judgement on the personality profile of your audience.

2. Match your communication content to the audience profile.

3. Use the Personality Guide to score the resulting communications, and adjust until a suitable match is obtained.

Watch the Marketing to Personality Types video at
http://www.espconsultancy.co.uk/marketing_to_personaility_types

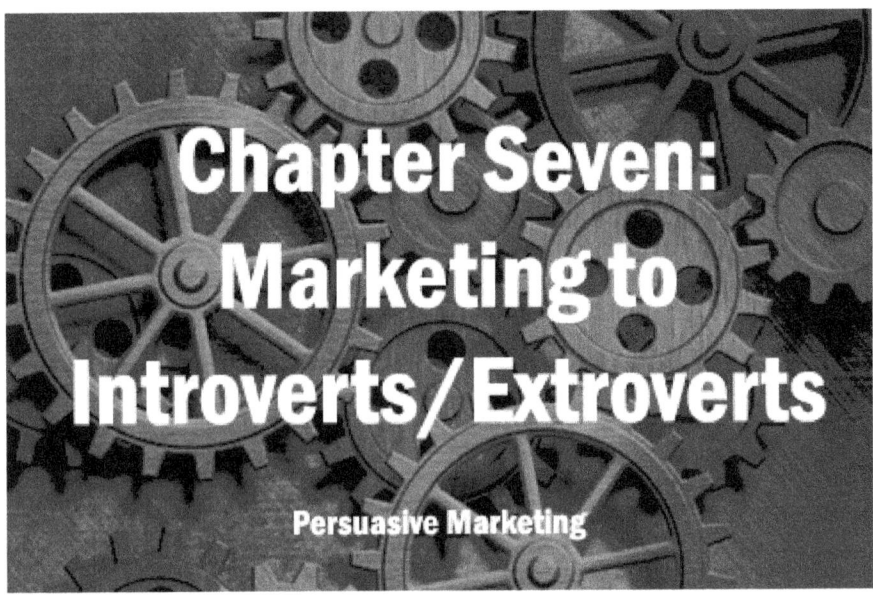

Introvert/Extrovert Personality Traits

The Introvert-Extrovert personality trait is useful because it tells us how people prefer to process information, specifically when making judgements on content and whether they believe it or not.

Introverts are not necessarily shy.

Shy people are anxious or frightened or self-excoriating in social settings; Introverts generally are not. Introverts use an internal frame of reference to process content, thoughts and ideas. They make value judgements based on their direct personal experience, beliefs and knowledge. They 'know their own mind' and are less likely to be influenced by overt sales tactics, claims or promises.

Introverts place great faith in their frame of reference and will often stick with it even though there appears to be credible evidence against. This can give others the impression that they are stubborn or in extreme cases unreasonable, but

Introverts would rather trust what they know rather than what they are told.

Extroverts are not necessarily sociable.

Extroverts are highly receptive and tuned-in with their environment, and are naturally responsive to people, which is what energises them.

Extroverts have an external frame of reference; they are more sensitive to, and more likely to consider the opinions of others. They are likely to make decisions that are driven by outside references and influences such as peer group, social or trend considerations. Often these influences could outweigh their personal judgements and experiences.

Extroverts are more likely than Introverts to be receptive to advertisers with whom they have no existing relationship.

Guide for marketing to Introverts/Extroverts

Unless the guide mentions both the behaviours, then it's appropriate to assume that what is true for one is the opposite for the other.

Introverts can be stubborn

Attempting to change the opinions or behaviour of an Introvert can be difficult, especially if they have already formed an opinion about your brand, product or service. In order to persuade them, consider messages that allow them to find the evidence themselves, or at least give the impression that they have, rather than just presenting them with it.

Covert forms of advertising work well to Introverts.

Social advertising works well to Extroverts.

Extroverts like recommendations

Marketing materials that rely on 3rd party recommendations, peer group pressure, social conforms or popular trends will influence this group. Especially if they can also join, conform or be a part of it.

Introverts tend not to value testimonials, unless they believe the source.

Extroverts tend to believe testimonials, especially from high profile people.

Introverts hate to be rushed.

So avoid hype and speed related offers, not only does it not work, it can have a negative effect. For the same reason do not expect an immediate purchase or change of behaviour to be made. Introverts need time to process information before making a decision, and will wait until they are sure before acting.

If you are conducting research, such as focus groups or interviews remember that Introverts think carefully about what they are going to say before it comes out of their mouths. If you do not give them enough time to think about their answer you will miss out on their insights, so give them a chance to respond before you move on.

Introverts: multi stage relationships with slower returns.

Extroverts: single stage relationships with fast returns.

Extroverts as advocates

Extroverts are comfortable recommending or passing on ideas to their large group of acquaintances, especially if they are part of a social networking group.

Introverts may not be comfortable recommending your product to people they don't know well, but can be surprisingly passionate about their experiences with the people they regard as close friends.

Use Introverts to share complex ideas/personal experiences with small tight knit groups.

Use Extroverts to share experience/gossip with everyone they know.

Introverts have little time for small talk

They tend to say what they mean and mean what they say.

Anything else would be 'fluffy', 'false' and viewed with suspicion.

Marketing communications should clearly and succinctly get to the point as quickly as possible.

Introverts: Be quick, be obvious, be direct.

Extroverts: Entertain them, amuse them confide in them.

Extroverts love phones and especially mobiles

It's good to talk is the ultimate Extrovert headline. If you phone an Extrovert and leave a message, expect a return call. After all, if they can avoid writing a letter, sending a text message or email they will.

Introverts respond better to Radio, Press, Mail and Email. Use response mechanisms that don't require interaction.

Extroverts respond better to Phone, Face-to-Face and In-store promotions. Use response mechanisms that have an element of interaction.

Introverts like to read.

People who read the entire communication tend to be introvert. Strategically placed advertisements in elevators, canteens, trains etc. are more likely to be read by Introverts.

For that reason, Introverts like to be given written information especially if they can read it in their own time, refer back to it and have time to think about it.

Introverts respond better to being provided with written information and being given time to react.

Extroverts respond better to verbal information and are comfortable making quick decisions.

Introverts are territorial and guard their personal space.

Introverts don't like interruptions and they really don't like surprises, uninvited visits or phone calls. No one encourages telemarketers but whereas Extroverts may complain but answer the phone anyway, Introverts will have their number delisted, join the TPS and turn the ringer off. Introverts have few qualms about hanging up on you or closing the door in your face. This is the reasoning: if you're uninvited and are rude enough to invade their private space you deserve all that you get.

Introverts – if you invade their space use indirect media e.g.: Direct Mail

Extroverts – if you join their group use interactive media e.g.: Social Networking.

Imagery that appeals to Extroverts.

Irrespective of the content of your imagery, certain rules apply for attracting Introverts and Extroverts.

Extroverts are naturally attracted to the way products interact with people and the effect they have.

So consider using people and ideally the more the merrier in your visuals. Because Extroverts are drawn to the product/people interaction, in practical terms this means having the product in the mid-ground as part of a scene, group or story.

Introverts prefer imagery that is 'the hero' and would find people distracting. Show the product in the fore-ground, ideally portrayed in a way that they can project into.

If using people to demonstrate the product or service, avoid showing faces to enable concentration of attention on the product or its benefit.

An example of an introvert advertisement

Introverts – close, little or no background, allow them to place themselves 'in the picture', if using people have them detached from main feature or use only parts such as hands.

An example of an extrovert advertisement

Watch the Marketing to Introvert/Extrovert video at
http://www.espconsultancy.co.uk/marketing_to_introvert_extrovert

Extroverts – place product as part of the story, mid-ground, reacting or getting a reaction from the surrounding people.

Copy styles that appeal to Introverts

Long copy works better for Introverts than short copy. For Introverts make the copy personal and use words like 'I' and 'you' and 'they' rather than 'we', 'us' and 'them'.

Acknowledge that they will require time to think something through rather than make a snap decision.

Response devices that appeal to Extroverts

The Extrovert needs a clear path to a personal connection where he/she can obtain the information. They favour response methods that include some form of personal interaction so 'start a conversation' with them.

The phone is most obvious, but forums and chat rooms work well.

The Introvert needs a path that doesn't require human interaction to obtain the information.

Introverts respond best with distanced interaction e.g. letter, email or website.

One response method for both personality traits will not maximise response.

Consider different response methods that will suit both Introverts and Extroverts.

Detailed/Big Picture Personality Traits

The "Detailed/Big Picture" (D/B) personality trait represents the way people exhibit preferences in the way they process information. Understanding the preferences of an audience in this respect gives marketers extremely valuable guidance on how best to structure communications. Specifically, it guides the amount of information included and the most appealing formats for the Content.

Those with a Detailed profile prefer to learn things in sequential steps; first this happens, then this, then this etc.

They prefer to deal in the facts and practicalities and will head for 'down to earth' details in preference to more abstract theories.

Being Detailed, they need communications that are to-the-point, clear and concise. They especially respond to examples, product demonstrations or concrete arguments.

They like to know the 'How', especially when it is supported by background information.

The Big Picture profile prefers to take new information and make sense of it by finding a trend or pattern. This profile is more concerned with ideas and theory than details. Being Big Picture, they prefer communications that provide the more abstract or global perspective.

They will not be overly interested in the detail, which they may find boring, unless they really have to. This group like to understand how the communication applies to them and like to explore the 'What If' possibilities it can offer.

If an audience is biased towards a Detailed profile, then the hot button is likely to be an immediate, tangible benefit.

If an audience is biased towards a Big Picture profile, then the hot button is likely to engage them with a vision, and offer help for them to make it a reality.

Constructing communication for Detailed/Big Picture audiences

The nature of the communication dictates the way that it is constructed. Traditionally, most communications start with low volumes of information that is more abstract and end with high volumes of information that is detailed.

Think of a classic brochure for example; the front cover will probably feature an image and a headline that describes the main benefit. An introductory spread will reiterate the main benefit or will place the subject matter in context. Right at the back of the brochure you are likely to find terms and conditions and graphs and charts.

The first is the front page, which typically has a Big Picture profile usually delivered by large areas of visual coverage and few words.

The content pages tend to be evenly split between Detailed and Big Picture and depending on the content the visual/copy ratio is also balanced.

And finally the information pages which might include terms and conditions, ordering details etc. are heavily biased towards a Detailed profile.

Because this is an established structure that people are familiar with, it works well for both Big Picture and Detailed profiles as everybody knows which part of a brochure they are headed for.

However, what should we do when we are creating a communication that has all the information contained in a single element? A press advertisement or a poster for example?

A Big Picture person faced with a poster or single page ad that is crammed full of information will just find it 'impenetrable' 'dull' or 'boring' and probably ignore it. And a Detailed person seeing a poster designed for a Big Picture audience may well view it as 'superficial', 'empty' or 'lightweight'.

Either way it is highly likely that they will unconsciously imprint their impression of the advertising brand with the same traits. The degree to which this will happen will be based on a number of factors; the personality difference between the viewer and the brand, the context in which they are exposed to the advertising and the frequency with which they are exposed to the advertising.

Some advertisers instinctively know this and create their brands to attract specific sectors of their marketplace.

The difference between Microsoft and Apple is a good example. Microsoft has a Detailed personality and a reputation for solid, no-nonsense, practical if not exciting products. Apple on the other hand are a Big Picture brand, their products when compared to Microsoft tend to be beautiful but less practical. But in truth, their Big Picture audience simply do not care; their association with products that they see as cool and stylish is more important, even when they are much more expensive than comparable products.

However, assuming that you wish to appeal to a broad spectrum of people and that you don't have an analysis of the audience Personality Traits to guide you there are really two options:

1. Create two different types of communication that will appeal to Big Picture and Detailed audiences respectively. This has the advantage of giving you two opportunities to capture attention, but runs the risk of diluting the overall impact of the campaign.

2. Try and appeal to both traits within one communication. Unless you decide to major on one trait with a 65/35 allocation of available space this is a compromise that rarely works. Instead, consider leading with the Big Picture message and offering a response mechanism that will satisfy the need for detail. Again, Detail people are accustomed to the convention that a Big Picture opener will lead them to the detail they require.

However, please note that this does not work the other way around. Big Picture people are rarely engaged by detail in order to have their need for an interesting idea satisfied later.

In the UK Marks and Spencer successfully combine 'Big Picture' generic T.V. brand advertising with product specific 'Detailed' promotions

Copy styles that appeal to a Detailed profile

This audience has a strong preference for structure and detail. Large amounts of copy will appeal to this group as they associate substance with volume. Because of this it is likely that they could perceive copy-light communications as superficial.

They will engage with copy presented in the form of lists, or broken down into small chunks of information. Stepped message techniques such as bullet points work well with this group.

Copy styles that appeal to Big Picture

This audience like concepts and ideas. If you can convey this in a picture that's perfect, otherwise use as few words as possible.

Small amounts of copy will appeal to this group as they are less likely to read copy-heavy communications, finding them 'boring'.

They are more likely to connect with copy that uses metaphor, stories or anecdotes, especially if they convey the ideas quickly and imaginatively.

Visual styles that appeal to Detailed

There is a distinct preference for charts, graphs and diagrams amongst this group. As a rule of thumb the more information they contain the more this group will value the content.

A 'Detailed' T.V commercial for the Hyundai range

Visual styles that appeal to Big Picture

There is a distinct preference for images that convey a story, concept or benefit amongst this group. Typically, the more abstract or unusual the images the more this group will relate to them.

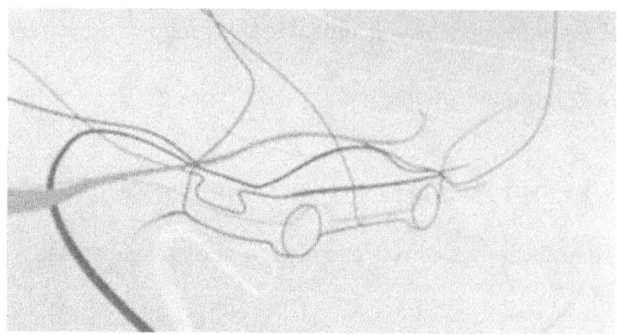

A 'Big Picture' T.V commercial for the AUDI A5

Watch the Marketing to Detailed/Big Picture video at
http://www.espconsultancy.co.uk/marketing_detailed_Big_Picture

Layouts that appeal to Detailed

This group are initially attracted to formal, structured layouts, rigid grid systems and information heavy styles. They engage with and tend to believe realistic photography over illustrations and will relate to close-up, cutaway images.

Detailed layout style

Layouts that appeal to Big Picture

This group are initially attracted to informal, unusual layouts, flexible grid systems and information light styles. They are more comfortable with drawings and illustrations over realistic photography especially if they communicate global or abstract themes.

Big Picture format style

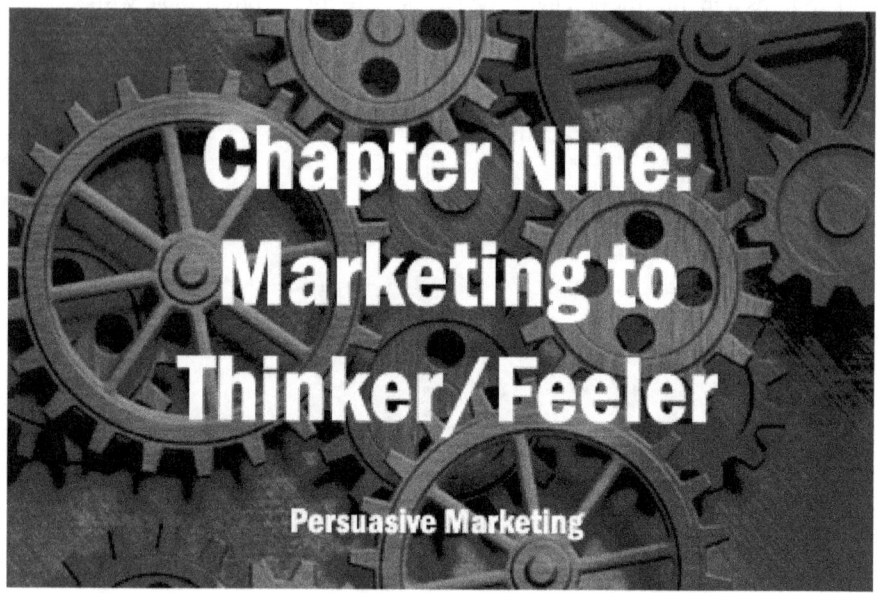

Thinker/Feeler Personality Traits

The "Thinking/Feeling (T/F) Personality Trait relates to our decision making preferences.

Typically, a Feeler is more likely to make decisions based upon convictions, while a Thinker is more likely to make decisions based upon logic. This is the one personality trait that does seem to have a gender bias.

Depending on the study it seems that 62-74% of women are Feelers, 26-38% Thinker. While 62-74% of men are Thinkers and 26-38% Feelers.

A Feeler is more likely to be subjective and deal better with emotive situations, while a Thinker is more likely to be objective, and prefers situations to be rational.

Thinker Feeler is a personality trait with a big impact on marketing decisions as Marketing is essentially the application of rational processes to understand emotional or intuitive responses.

Persuading a Thinker

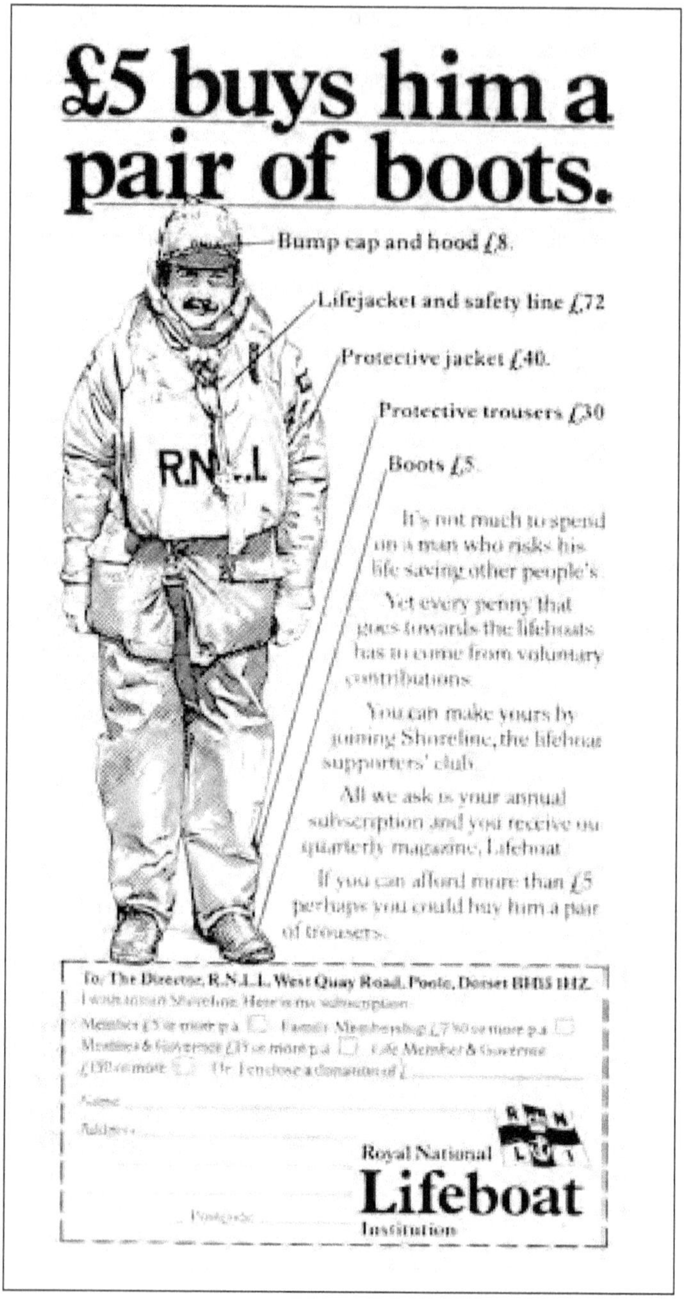
£5 buys him a pair of boots.
Bump cap and hood £8.
Lifejacket and safety line £72
Protective jacket £40.
Protective trousers £30
Boots £5.
R.N.L.I.
It's not much to spend on a man who risks his life saving other people's.
Yet every penny that goes towards the lifeboats has to come from voluntary contributions.
You can make yours by joining Shoreline, the lifeboat supporters' club.
All we ask is your annual subscription and you receive our quarterly magazine, Lifeboat.
If you can afford more than £5 perhaps you could buy him a pair of trousers.
To: The Director, R.N.L.I., West Quay Road, Poole, Dorset BH15 1HZ.
Royal National
Lifeboat
Institution

Left brained, 'Thinker' product advertising tends to focus on specific details rather than its benefits or effects.

Thinkers make their decisions based on objective criteria and believe that emotions must be subjugated to the situation, while Feelers make decisions based on how they will affect the people involved. The T/F preference is one of the most difficult to explain and resolve. Fortunately, it is the easiest one to recognize in everyday life.

What is apparent is the way that this personality trait correlates particularly well with certain professions. Feelers are predominant in people-oriented fields; the world of business on the other hand, is dominated by Thinkers.

Brands and products naturally fall into Thinker/Feeler Personality Profiles. Often this is dictated by the nature of the product and is then reflected in the advertising. A couple of good examples of Feeler advertising are shown later for Andrex and Cadbury's Dairy Milk.

The Thinker advertising for Tesco Finance and Money Supermarket does carry more information relative to the Feeler ads but what distinguishes them as Thinker ads is the rational argument, objective layout and reliance on specific, factual data.

Thinkers often need time to make decisions because they want to understand the risk involved and if necessary may well want measures in place to minimise them. Therefore, because Thinkers tend to be more control-driven, any advertising to them will need to appreciate to Thinkers:

1. Need a detailed understanding of the process used to make a recommendation and the process they might use to arrive at a decision.

2. Have an appetite for information

3. Prefer hard, substantiated data especially if supported by independent rigorous research

4. Must analyse the pros and cons before making a decision.

5. Proceed with caution without betraying their feelings.

6. Will rarely be persuaded by emotional arguments, preferring to trust in reason and logic.

Overall, Thinkers will need to be satisfied that the facts have been lined up and examined one-by-one. Once all options have been thoroughly explored and they have had time to digest all the information then they will be ready to reach a decision. This is why they prefer structured, chronological arrangements of content because it enables them to follow the logic of the argument.

A good Thinker structure for advertising is:

Define the problem

Describe and evaluate the options

Explain why yours is best

Assess the value or benefit of that option

Provide a logical next step

Copy Content

This audience prefers copy in short sentences, of which ideally, 70% should be less than 12 words long. They will engage and respond well to logical words and appreciate a direct, formal and factual style. Avoid the use of feeling based words and phrases as this might make the copy seem overly emotive and sentimental. Copy written in the third person would be particularly effective with this group.

Persuading a Feeler

Andrex and Cadbury's are positioned as 'Feeler' brands. Virgin often uses feeler style ads to build its perception as a 'Feeler' brand.

Watch the Marketing to Thinker/Feeler video at

http://www.espconsultancy.co.uk/marketing_to_thinker_feeler

Feelers tend to make quick decisions because they are largely based on their gut-reaction. Feelers tend to be more socially driven. Often they just need to get a sense of the impact the decision will have on those involved and they will instinctively feel the right answer.

Any advertising to Feelers should recognise that Feelers:

- Need to appreciate how their decision might impact on others

- Have a sense of connection

- Prefer the emotional arguments

- Must have an empathy before making a decision

- Proceed quickly once engaged

- Will not be persuaded by reason and logic alone, preferring to trust their feelings and emotions

Overall Feelers will want to know the story behind the decision. How it might affect them and how that will impact on their feelings. This is why they prefer content rich in stories, personal opinions and metaphors; it enables them to 'get under the skin' of the argument.

A good Feeler structure for advertising is:

- Describe how the product makes people feel

- Tell the story

- Using testimonials

- Explain what their decision will mean

- And the impact of positive decision

Copy Content

This audience prefers copy that uses longer sentences. They will empathise and engage with feeling based words and will connect with a descriptive, flowing and personal style. Avoid the use of logical words as they might make the copy seem cold and impersonal. Copy written in the first person would be particularly effective with this group.

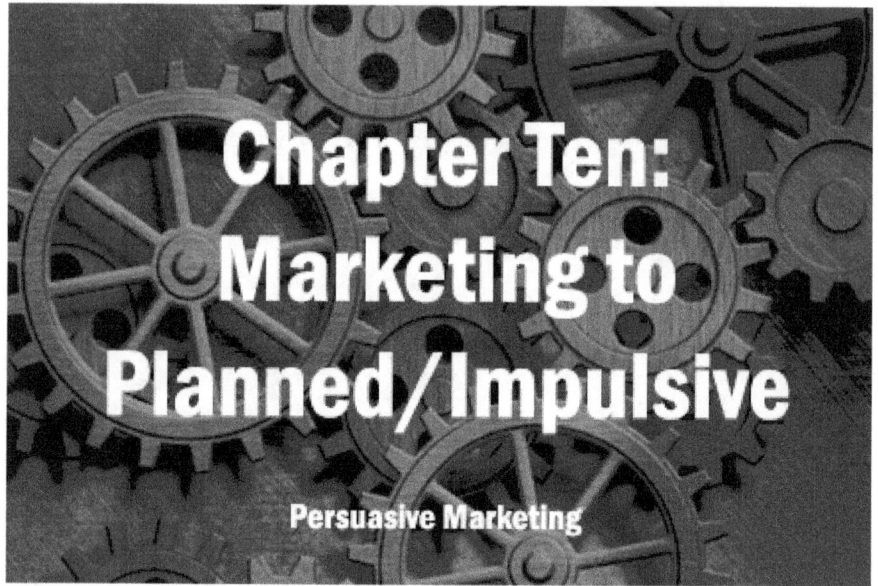

Planned/Impulsive Personality Traits

The "Planned/Impulsive (P/I) Personality Trait relates to our needs for closure or flexibility.

While this may well be the shortest of the personality trait topics, if some form of response or action is the purpose of your advertising then this may be the most important of all. That's because the Planned/Impulsive personality trait determines the probability of action, and the type of action that will be taken.

Clearly, this is particularly relevant to Marketing when we are considering how to close the sale or indeed trigger any kind of action or response. In those situations and instances, people's preferences for Planned/Impulsive are of major significance in determining whether you will get the result you want or not.

The Planned Profile

The press ad for BBC Radio 6 and the Credit and DVLA television all appeal to the planned personality profile.

Watch the Marketing to Planned/Impulsive video at

http://www.espconsultancy.co.uk/marketing_to_planned_impulsive

The Planned trait refers to a person's innate desire to bring closure to things, to make a decision, to leave no loose ends.

The Planned Personality trait is more resistant to sudden change and prefers regular or consistent patterns in their habits and behaviours. They have a high need for closure, sequence and structure. Typically they are more eager to make a decision, to move forward, and to have things settled.

The Planned profile's instinct, assuming you have addressed their needs, is to move steadily toward a close, though an

Impulsive will probably regard this as procrastinating, tedious and inflexible.

When closing people with a Planned personality trait, you may just need to point the way and leave them to it.

Planners make considered purchases and will often buy early to secure their choice as purchasing early in the buying cycle serves their preference for predictability and certainty.

The Step or Check List Offer

Any offer that is presented in a sequential manner will engage with the Planned profile. Variations of this 'check list' offer are very common, so adapt the structure to be appropriate to your product, service or Brand.

The key to the technique is to highlight the main benefits as a list. Then add the ordering process and a future benefit.

Charities use this technique very successfully in the form of a questionnaire which ends with a donation form.

An excellent and very useful construction for the Step or Check List offer is:

Five good reasons why you should buy today

1 – Benefit A. The main reason for purchase

2 – Benefit B. Secondary reason for purchase

3 – Benefit C. Secondary reason for purchase

4 – Place Order. Show or detail the physical

response device or mechanism

5 – Post order benefit. The benefit of having

taken action

To close this group make sure that the step-by-step process of what they should do and what will happen when they do it, is sufficiently detailed.

The Impulsive Profile

Not surprisingly, the opposite is true of the Impulsive personality trait; instinctively they wish to keep their options open. The term impulsive is commonly associated with rapid, spur-of-the-moment decisions and a Planned person may view an Impulsive's decisions as ill-considered and rushed, but this is not because the Impulsive processes decisions with ease or complacency.

Without the sequential structure of the Planned, for the Impulsive, making a decision means a restriction of options and possibilities and they will avoid it if at all possible. They are less driven to closure, to a decision, preferring to weigh the options and keep things open.

Expect them to resist being locked in.

Don't pressure them to make a decision as they will resist any premature attempts to close.

They will often make impulsive decisions, in terms of being 'ill-considered and rushed', because they have either left the decision to the last minute, they perceive that their options are running out, or they perceive that making a decision is the only way to keep their options open.

That said they will take as long as you give them to make a decision so you do need some form of leverage.

Although not ideal, the only strategy that seems to work with this group is to imply that by waiting they are in fact restricting their options. For example, time limited and quantity restricted offers tend to work well with this personality trait.

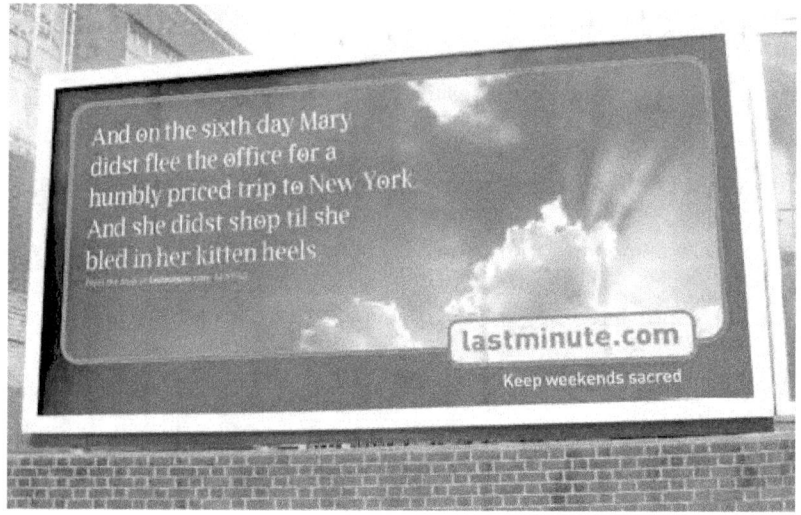

Lastminute.com (above top) is the archetypal 'Impulsive' brand. Many messages like the recruitment ad above are aimed at the impulsive personality.

Closing Patterns for the Impulsive Profile

'Trial' or 'Puppy Dog' offers.

This style of offer works because of once the product has been used, or

in the case of the puppy held, it becomes harder to give back. This enables the

Impulsive to keep their options open as it allows them to use the product or service for a specified period of time with the understanding that they will make a commitment after the trial period.

The concept here is that they will become familiar with it, increasing the probability of a positive outcome.

Examples of Trial offers:

"Buy today, nothing to pay for six months."

"Three month free trial"

"Try before you buy."

"Free Samples."

Restrictive offers.

Restrictive offers give a reason for a decision now, because something will change which will affect and restrict the Impulsive person's ability to keep their options open. As long as the offer has a sense of urgency then this is a very effective technique to use with this profile.

The construction of this argument is quite simple: (take action) before (the restriction)

Here are some examples:

"Buy now because tomorrow the price increases."

"That's the last one we have but I have two other purchasers interested."

"The two-for-one ends today"

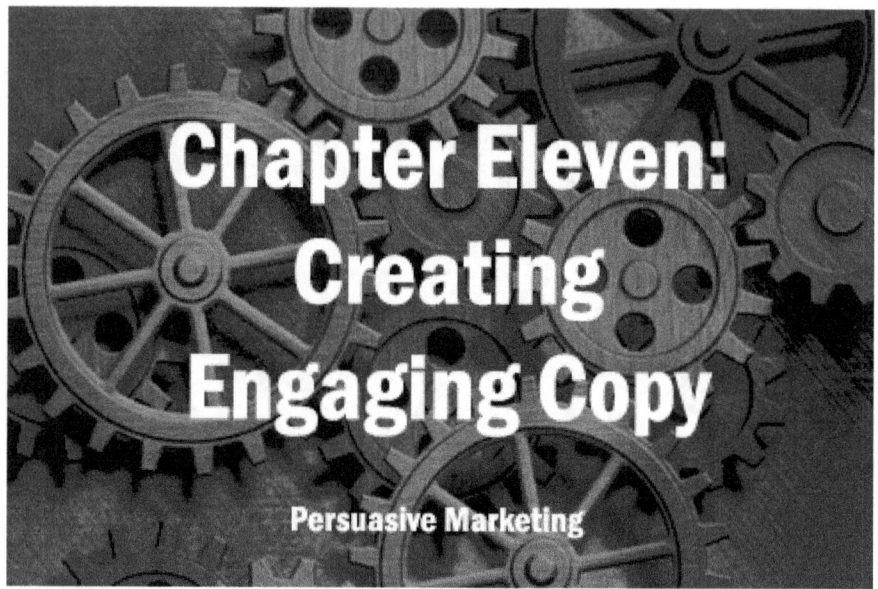

We represent our world internally using information from our external senses of sight, touch, sound, smell and taste. The combination of these five senses enables our brain to create what we perceive as the world around us. The five senses are constantly transmitting data to the brain, although we tend to pay attention to one sense more than others depending on what we are doing. For example, in an art gallery we are more likely to pay attention to the information from our eyes, in a concert our ears and when eating taste.

In fact developing a specific sense is often a critical skill needed to pursue a career. A chef needs a discriminating palate; a musician a fine ear; an artist an eye for colour; a physiotherapist a sensitive touch and a perfumer the nose for a bouquet.

In NLP terms, the five senses are called Representational Systems because that is how we re-present the external world into our internal model. They act as filters that shape our experience.

An understanding of representational systems and how they shape communication is a pre-requisite for marketing professionals because all communication starts with a thought. Then we use Content, Tone of Voice and Body Language to convey those thoughts to others.

But what are thoughts?

One way to describe thinking is that we consciously or unconsciously recall the sights, sounds, feelings, tastes and smells that we have experienced and use those memories as the raw material, the building blocks to create and express new thoughts. This is such an instinctive process that we do it unconsciously, we tend to focus on what we are thinking about rather than how the thought is constructed.

Understanding this construction is useful from a marketing perspective because when we communicate we tend to have a distinct preference for one or perhaps two representational systems regardless of what we are communicating. If you know the preference of your audience when communicating with them you can quickly gain a deep level of rapport simply by using their language constructions.

Many people can make clear mental images and think mainly in pictures. Others find this viewpoint difficult. They may talk to themselves a good deal while others base their actions mostly on their feel for a situation. When a person tends to use one internal sense habitually, this is called their preferred or primary system. This simply means that they are likely to be more discriminating and able to make finer distinctions in this system than in the others.

This is one reason why some people are naturally better, or 'talented', at particular tasks or skills. They have learned to become more adept at using one or two internal senses and these have become smooth and practised, running without effort or awareness. Things just come 'naturally' to them. The flip side is that the other representational systems will be not so well developed. This will make certain skills more difficult or less 'natural'. For example, playing a musical instrument well is difficult without the ability to hear sounds internally.

Evelyn Glennie, is a world class percussionist who mastered her art whilst being profoundly deaf. Although her hearing did not work very well, she was always able to 'hear' sounds inside her head.

Dominance in one system is not better in an absolute sense than another, but it will influence what you can do well.

Athletes need a well-developed kinaesthetic awareness, and it would be difficult to be a successful graphic designer without a talent for making clearly constructed mental pictures.

One skill shared by outstanding performers in any field is to be able to move easily through all the representational systems and use the most appropriate one for the task in hand.

The same is true for marketing professionals as communication styles of different Brands, products and services show distinct representation system bias. Often this is dictated by the audience that they are targeted at, sometimes it happens by accident and ideally it is because of a conscious desire to gain rapport between the Brand, product or service and a specific audience.

Language and representational systems

We use language to communicate our thoughts so it is not surprising that the words we use reflect the way we think.

One of the co-founders of NLP, John Grinder tells of the time when Richard Bandler (the other co-founder) was laughing about someone who had said, *'I see what you are saying.'*

'Think about it literally,' he said. *'What could they possibly mean?'*

'Well,' said John, *'Let's take it literally; suppose it means that they are making images of the meaning of the words that you use.'*

This was an interesting idea which prompted the first experiment in understanding the effect of representational systems on rapport.

At their next seminar, they took green, yellow and red cards and had attendees describe their purpose for being there.

Those who used a lot of words and phrases to do with feelings got a yellow card. Those who used a lot of words and phrases to do with hearing and sounds got green cards.

Those who used words and phrases predominantly to do with seeing got red cards.

Then Grinder and Bandler conducted a simple experiment. In groups of two, people with the same colour card were asked to sit down and talk together for five minutes. Then they were asked to sit down and talk to somebody with a different colour card. The differences that were observed in rapport between the two groups were profound. People with the same colour cards had much higher levels of rapport than the mixed colour groups.

Since that first simple experiment, it has been replicated many times always with the same result – groups that use the same representational systems in language have greater rapport than those that do not.

This bank of knowledge forms the basis of the use of predicates to measure engaging language.

Predicates

We use words to describe our thoughts, so our choice of words will indicate which representational system we are using. Consider four people who have just been exposed to the same communication.

The first might point out that they saw a lot in it, the examples were well chosen to illustrate the subject and it was written in a sparkling style.

The second might connect with the tone; it had a chatty prose style. In fact, they liked what they heard and would like to hear more.

The third feels it dealt with a weighty subject in a balanced way. That it touched on all the key topics, helping them to grasp its ideas easily.

The fourth understood the logic of the argument. The direct factual style enabled them to analyse its content objectively.

They all experienced the same communication. Yet you will notice that each person expressed themselves about the communication in a different way.

Regardless of what they thought about it, how they thought about it was different. One was thinking in pictures, the second in sounds, the third in feelings and the last logically.

These sensory-based words, adjectives, adverbs and verbs, are called predicates in NLP literature. Habitual use of one kind of predicate will indicate a person's preferred representational system.

For all practical purposes this is where the theoretical use of representational systems in NLP and their practical use in marketing diverge slightly.

Whist there are indeed five senses, in practice, only three score highly as dominant representational preferences.

In research conducted by ESP on over 40,000 people worldwide – the largest research group of its kind – we found that the preferred representational system for the research sample was:

29% Visual

28% Kinaesthetic

11% Auditory

Olfactory and Gustatory both scored less than 2%

At this point you may be wondering why the figures above don't add up to 100%. That's because during the research it was identified that a large percentage of the audience used a mixture of predicates which was dominated by logical language. This is termed auditory-digital in NLP.

Although logical language is not strictly speaking a true representational system because it is not derived from one of the five senses, it does indicate a way of structuring the thought process and therefore a way to gain rapport with an audience. In the research, 32% of those interviewed had a preference for Logical so it is now included as a 'representational system' in marketing applications

Using Predicates in analysis of Communications

It is possible to identify the preferred representational system of any Brand, Product or Service by paying attention to the language used in its marketing. General or mass market brands tend to use a rich and varied mix of predicates, using all the representational systems equally, hence their universal appeal.

You may like to become aware over the coming weeks what sort of words you favour in normal conversation. It is also fascinating to listen to others and discover what sort of sensory-based language they prefer.

Those of you who prefer to think in pictures may like to see if you can identify the colourful language patterns.

If you think kinesthetically, you could get in touch with the way people put themselves over.

If you think in sounds, listen carefully and tune in to how different people talk.

Or if you think logically, understand, analyse and comprehend the language of others.

Then it is easy to make the leap, see differently, get and feel for or compute the predicates in marketing communications and how slight changes to them dramatically change their structure.

As with all good communication, the secret is not so much what you say, but how you say it. To create rapport, match predicates with the audience. You will be speaking their language, and presenting ideas in just the way they think about them.

Your ability to do this will depend on two things:

First; your ability to appreciate the preferences of your audience.

Secondly; an adequate vocabulary of predicates to connect with them.

You are more likely to gain rapport with an audience who connect with the predicates used, regardless of whether you personally prefer them or not. If you are not sure of the preferences of your audience it is a good idea to use a good mix of predicates.

Let those with a visual preference see what you are saying.

Let the auditory types hear you loud and clear, structure messages that let the feelers in the audience grasp your meaning and make sense for those that are logical.

Otherwise why would they listen to you? You risk between 68%-89% of your audience not connecting with your message should your communications be written in one predicate style.

Now let us deal with the practicalities of using predicates to engage and connect with an audience.

Although it is not taught in this way to aspiring copywriters, it's a surprisingly easy discipline to learn and will have a big impact on the copy produced. It also provides a structure to avoid many of the common frustrations changes or delays that are all too common in the creative process. That's because even before the final copy is approved, the misuse of predicates is responsible for a large percentage of rewrites and amendments which cause delays, friction and additional expense.

For example, have you ever been in a position of evaluating copy that may be factually correct yet you have not felt comfortable with the 'tone' or 'style', but couldn't quite articulate why?

If so, then it is highly likely that the majority of predicates used were not from your preferred representational system(s).

Or have you approved copy only for it to come back from another stakeholder with numerous style rather than factual corrections? Again it is the mismatch of predicates that is most likely to be responsible.

An understanding of the effect of predicates can nullify many of these problems before they start. The starting point is to be able to recognise the four predicate types. As a rule of thumb, any sensory based words could be classed as predicates. Although by no means exhaustive, below is a listing of commonly used predicates in advertising, for each of the four main representational systems.

Predicate Directory

Visual Predicates

See, look, appear, view, show, dawn, reveal, envision, illuminate, twinkle, clear, foggy, focused, hazy, crystal, flash, imagine, picture, sparkling, snap shot, vivid, perceive, light, ray, mesmerise, watch, perspective, frame, shine, dim, image, vision, observe, dark, watch, reveal, illusion, shine, reflect, clarify, notice, focus.

Auditory Predicates

Hear, listen, sound(s), make music, harmonise, tune in/out, be all ears, ring, silence, be heard, resonate, deaf, dissonance, overtones, unhearing, attune, outspoken, tell, announce, talk, speak, resonate, state, whine, babble, echo, orchestrate, whisper, snap, hum, loud, dialogue, say, shout, quiet.

Kinaesthetic Predicates

Feel , touch, grasp, get hold of, slip through, catch on, tap into, make contact, throw out, turn around, hard, unfeeling, concrete, scrape, get a handle, solid, suffer, un budging, impression, touch base, rub, smooth, pushy, stumble, in touch, relaxed, loose, cool, tepid, heavy, push, warm, gentle, pressure, tension.

Logical Predicates

Analyse, sense, experience, understand, think, learn, process, decide, motivate, consider, evaluate, change, perceive, insensitive, examine, distinct, conceive, know, question, rational, be conscious, logic, reasonable, statistically.

To dramatically change the tone or style of copy all that is required is to:

Change the frequency of predicates.

Higher numbers of predicates make copy more friendly, informal and personal. Lower numbers make copy official, formal and impersonal.

Change the types of predicates used.

Disproportionate use of one type of predicate will appeal more to those with that representational system preference.

This is fine if it is known that an audience has a preference, otherwise it is better to have a balanced predicate use.

In reality the audience will not be aware of predicate usage, yet at an unconscious level it is one of the factors that will prompt them to engage or not with the copy. Notice how the use of different predicates changes the style of the example paragraph below.

It is quite possible that one version will look right, feel better, sound good or make sense dependant on your own predicate preferences. One will be less engaging even though the basic content, structure and facts remain the identical.

This is the original paragraph as it was printed with the predicates highlighted in bold.

*IT'S EASIER THAN YOU MIGHT **THINK** TO MAKE A DIFFERENCE.*

*As well as receiving regular emails packed full of useful saving tips and advice, you'll also get access our dedicated Advice Line, where you'll be able to **ask** our expert advisers any questions you may have.*

It uses a Logical predicate in the headline and an Auditory predicate in the body copy. But perhaps you might connect more with the same paragraph structure with a Kinaesthetic bias.

*IT'S EASIER THAN YOU MIGHT **FEEL** TO MAKE A DIFFERENCE.*

*As well as **catching** regular emails packed full of useful saving tips and advice, you'll also be able to **tap** into our dedicated Advice Line, where you'll be able to **contact** our expert advisers with any questions you may have.*

For some people the same structure paragraph with a Visual bias will make everything crystal clear.

*IT'S EASY FOR YOU TO **SEE** HOW TO MAKE A DIFFERENCE.*

*As well as revealing regular, **colourful** emails packed full of useful saving tips and advice, you'll also **view** our dedicated Advice Line, where our expert advisers will **reveal** answers to any questions you may **imagine**.*

Some people will resonate more with a paragraph structure with an Auditory bias.

*IT'S EASY FOR YOU TO **SPEAK** OUT AND MAKE A DIFFERENCE.*

*As well as **hearing** from us via regular emails of useful saving tips and advice, you can also **chat** to our dedicated Advice Line, where you'll be able to **ask** our expert advisers any questions you may have.*

And some will only consider it makes sense when analysing a paragraph structure with a Logical bias.

*IT'S EASIER THAN YOU MIGHT **THINK** TO MAKE A DIFFERENCE.*

*As well as **evaluating** regular emails packed full of useful saving tips and advice, you'll also **experience** our dedicated Advice Line, where you'll be able to **question** our expert advisers on any queries you may have.*

The important thing to notice in this exercise is that each paragraph will appear, evaluate, feel or resonate in a slightly different way, and this difference is purely a result of changing the predicates. Notice also that all of the predicates used were simply picked from the directory above and where possible dropped into the existing text.

Applying Predicates

Use this technique for making changes to copy if you know the representational preferences of your audience.

1. Check the text for existing predicates – manually run through the text highlighting predicate types and number or input the text through a benchmarketing analysis system for an accurate count.

2. Compare the count against the audience profile – specifically you are looking for a match or similarity between the type and frequency of predicates used.

3. Amend as necessary – the object is to match the audience profile. Specifically ensure that any predicates contained within headlines or subheads are of the right type.

4. Chart or plot the changes against the audience profile – this applies research to the creative process and provides a degree of process and rigor to support the existing copy style. In addition it reduces the likelihood of other stakeholders changing the text to suit their preferences.

If you don't know the audience representational preferences then:

Use a balance of predicates based on the generic research, 32% logical, 29% visual, 28% kinaesthetic and 11% auditory, ideally using a mix of different preferences in headlines and sub-heads. The percentages provide a useful guideline but the important thing is to include something for everybody.

For example the text used in the previous example if balanced to include the four predicate styles, may have read something like this...

*IT'S EASIER THAN YOU MIGHT **THINK** TO MAKE A DIFFERENCE.*

*As well as **hearing** from us via regular emails of useful saving tips and advice, you'll also be able to **tap** into our dedicated Advice Line, where our expert advisers will **reveal** answers to any questions you may have.*

Finally, before you start to analyse or change copy for your business, consider undertaking the three exercises below, which are designed to help you become more familiar with the use of predicates.

Predicate Exercise One

To practice inserting predicates into text try this simple exercise before moving on to your own copy. By using predicates from the Predicate Directory complete the sentence below to appeal to an audience profile that is

50% Logical

25% Visual

25% Kinaesthetic

0% Auditory

You might _____ that all brands are the

same, but now _____ the facts review the

evidence and _____ if this brand _____

right for you.

Now, undertake the exercise again using a different selection of

predicate words.

You might _____ that all brands are the

same, but now _____ the facts review the

evidence and _____ if this brand _____

right for you.

Finally, undertake the exercise again choosing a different selection of

predicate words.

You might _____ that all brands are the

same, but now _____ the facts review the

evidence and _____ if this brand _____

right for you.

This exercise is good for helping you get used to thinking about copy in this way. Ideally undertake this exercise with a number of colleagues, compare results and notice the difference subtle changes to the predicates make to the copy style.

Predicate Exercise Two

Now by using predicates from the Predicate Directory complete the sentence below to appeal to an audience profile that is:

25% Logical

25% Visual

25% Kinaesthetic

25% Auditory

You might _____ that all brands are the

same, but now _____ the facts review the

evidence and _____ if this brand _____

right for you.

Now, undertake the exercise again using a different selection of predicate words.

You might _____ that all brands are the

same, but now _____ the facts review the

evidence and _____ if this brand _____

right for you.

Finally, undertake the exercise again choosing a different selection of predicate words.

You might _____ that all brands are the

same, but now _____ the facts review the

evidence and _____ if this brand _____

right for you.

Predicate Exercise Three

Take something you have written previously (min 120 words) and identify:

The type of predicates used.

The frequency of predicates used.

Ideally this should be something that you have written in an informal, personal style as it is likely to contain more predicates. Emails to friends or work colleagues would be good for this exercise. If you do not have something that is 120 words long then it is perfectly valid to take two or three shorter pieces and add them together.

The percentage of each predicate type used will give an indication of your own preferences. Once identified, consciously replace the predicates with some from your least favoured representation system. This exercise will increase your range and enable you to become more flexible and able to better connect with more of your audience, more of the time.

Watch the Creating Engaging Copy video at

http://www.espconsultancy.co.uk/creating_engaging_copy

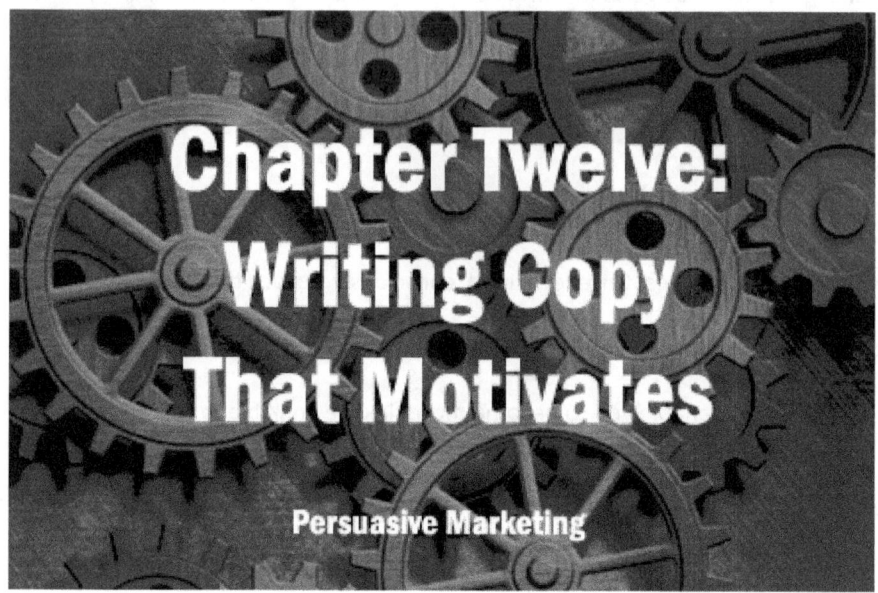

Let's get down to basics. How about life and death?

How can you tell whether something or someone is alive or dead? Assuming you ever need to. Well signs of movement are a good sign. If we have to determine whether something or someone is alive or dead we instinctively look for movement; action and behaviour. Life signs such as pulse and breathing are a good start but the real convincer is when they get up and start moving around.

So if there is life, and there is action, the next question is; what affects or modifies that action?

Clearly, there will be different forces or influences that can drive or incentivise that movement and actions. We can call them Motivations.

Definitions of Motivation from Merriam-Webster's Medical Dictionary

A motivating force, stimulus, or influence

(as a drive or incentive)

Inner or social stimulus for an action

Now from a marketing perspective, having an audience that is alive is a good start because we probably want them, at some stage, to move, take action and do something. The issue usually is how we influence them to take an action or take on a belief that is helpful to us and our objectives.

The way we express actions or activities is with verbs; what my Primary School teacher used to call 'doing words'.

Definition of a verb: a word (part of speech) that conveys action or a state of being

Every aspect of our lives is described and structured with verbs. Even if you exclude the verb 'to be', you still find that the vast majority of all the sentences ever written include at least one verb; they are fundamental to how we think about and describe our world and our lives:

I *think*, therefore I am

I *have* a dream

Spider Pig, Spider Pig, *does* whatever a Spider Pig *does*

So verbs are very important. Imagine if you had to express yourself or describe something without having them in your vocabulary.

Imagine if you wanted to encourage students to attend University of and there were no words such as; look, click, enquire, respond, apply, listen, fill out, join, visit, call, discover, come, try, sign up, give, study, learn, enjoy, qualify, graduate and benefit.

So if verbs are so important in structuring our experience, suggestions and intentions, the next question is; can they have a different effect on an audience if they are framed or modified in some way?

Most people are aware that verbs can be described by words we label adverbs.

Definition of an adverb: a word or group of words that serves to modify a whole sentence, a verb, another adverb, or an adjective.

This means that wherever we use our very-important verbs, we are likely to be modifying or qualifying them with words that express some relation of place, time, manner, attendant circumstance, degree, cause, inference, result, condition, exception, concession, purpose, or means.

Effectively the adverbs are answering the questions how? In what way?, when? where?, and to what extent?

I often visit the seaside

We were happily married for eight months.

Unfortunately, we were married for four and a half years

To boldly go (split infinitive oh dear!)

So adverbs qualify and add commentary and useful information to the verb.

However, there is another way to modify a verb. This is a way that is so powerful; it can actually set the context for the verb before you even find out what the verb is.

This way uses other verbs - a specific set of verbs – to express the speaker's or writer's attitude toward the action or state given by the main verb.

This means that this specific set of verbs – known as Modal Operators – can be used to influence and direct the degree of necessity, obligation, permission, determination or willingness associated with the main verb.

In today's marketing climate, it would be hard to justify expenditure that did not have the potential for a healthy return on that investment. Typically there are three elements to writing copy that encourages that return; make it engaging, make it motivating and make it persuasive.

Having taken the first step and engaged an audience with the appropriate use of predicates as described in earlier, then the next step must be to motivate them into taking action.

The Sequence of Motivation and NLP

NLP was founded in the studious monitoring of the way people speak to one another in everyday conversation but particularly in the language patterns used by eminent and successful psycho-therapists. Those professional practitioners had demonstrated an ability to help people by influencing their beliefs and behaviours – even when they had never systematically explained what it was they were doing.

When those language patterns were noted and codified not only could the researchers recognise familiar words and commonly used expressions they were also able to organise them in a form that revealed the systematic relationship they have with each other.

And, from a more practical point of view, as we accept the power those language patterns can have to influence and direct people's thinking, we can think in a totally different way about how we use them to make our own copy better structured and specifically in this Module, more capable of generating motivation and influencing behaviour.

As in the rest of this book, these elements of language are not new inventions and they haven't just been dreamed up by NLP. They are fixed action patterns, forms and structures that have always been there and always been used by all of us. Some people you may have dealt with in the past will already have been better than others at using Modal Operators; whether they realised why or not. They may have done so instinctively or they may have read or been taught that certain phrases or scripts produce a desired effect and simply re-used them parrot-like.

The difference now is that you will have the option to use those forms and structures thoughtfully and deliberately in any context and medium you choose. And of course, when another speaker or writer is using Modal Operators you will be able to identify them.

Modal Operators – the key to motivating copy

A Modal Operator is a verb that modifies another verb, so it is always followed by another verb:

"I can't believe you said that"

"I have to work"

"I will become successful."

A Modal Operator is a "mode of operating" - a way of being in the world and relating to part of it, or all of it. A Modal Operator modulates our experience of much (or all) of what we do in very important ways.

Sometimes, a person says simply, "I can't," or "I have to", or "I will"; as communicating the mode is the most important thing and the actual content is specified by the context.

Since a verb always describes an activity or process, a Modal Operator is a verb that modifies how an activity is done. An adverb sometimes precedes the verb it is modifying and sometimes follows it. A Modal Operator always precedes it and this is part of the power of a Modal Operator.

A Modal Operator sets a general orientation or global direction before we even know what the activity is.

Specifically, Modal Operators are auxiliary verbs that express an attitude or orientation regarding the degree of necessity, obligation, permission, determination, willingness, probability or ability.

We categorise these special verbs into six areas of attitude, activity and orientation and here is an illustrative list of them that you could place in front of any main verb:

Modal Operator - Label (of Orientation)

1. I can't - Negative Possibility

2. I couldn't - Negative Probability

3. I mustn't - Negative Necessity

4. I must - Necessity

5. I could - Probability

6. I can   - Possibility

As you may notice, the top half is almost a mirror image of the bottom half with a sort of 'turnaround' between them. So moving through them from numbers one to six, the 'states of orientation' go from; a state of absolute refusal or inability; through a qualified refusal; and then restraint. This then turns around into; a state of 'having to'; through a qualified agreement; and finally to a state of willingness and determination.

That sequence reflects the transition from a state of negativity to positivity:

1. from the extreme of an outright refusal or inability

I won't buy it

2. through refusal for a reason

I couldn't buy it because I have no money

3. being restrained

I mustn't buy it, I'll be in trouble

4. being compelled

I have to buy it whatever the consequences

5. agreement but …

I could buy it, but I will be short until the end of the month

6. to willing and able

I will buy it

A Modal Operator can modulate our experience of much (or all) of what we do in very important ways. Think of any activity, and describe it in a brief phrase, such as "looking out of the window" or "going to work". Now, use that phrase in each of the six Modal Operator areas:

I can't look out of the window

I wouldn't look out of the window

I mustn't look out of the window

I have to look out of the window

I could look out of the window

I will look out of the window

Never mind 'looking out of the window'; notice how your experience changes with each sentence, notice where your attention goes, and how you feel even when the content (the main verb) remains the same.

A Modal Operator can precede any verb and even before we know what that verb is, we know a great deal about the 'state' it is operating in.

For example, if someone says; "I just wouldn't ...." Before they give us the content, the main verb, we already know the 'state' they are operating in:

there is something which in other circumstances they might do - but for some reason they're not.

So the fact that the Modal Operator is largely independent of the content and context is what makes them such a powerful tool in our armoury. It could prompt the reader or listener towards a Probability or open them up to the Possibility.

Their power is in the suggestion they make even before we know what the action or activity is. Modal Operators provide copy with a direction and a momentum that moves the reader towards the desired action.

Suppose you want to broadcast a message that encourages a particular behaviour:

- You can buy this now

If someone's response to that is:

- I can't buy this now

there is clearly a gulf between those two states (1 and 6) and simply repeating:

- Yes you can buy this now

Is not going to make much difference, other than break rapport or cause annoyance. So here we start to think of the Modal Operators as links in a bridge that crosses that gulf.

Clearly, when you are writing copy for written or spoken messaging and you want to motivate the audience to particular actions and behaviours then moving them from states 1 to 3 – "I can't, shouldn't or mustn't" – is a good thing.

However, the real goal is actually to move them all the way to state 6 – "I can and I will".

A modal operator frames our experience in subtle yet important ways. Below are three sentences; say each to yourself, and become aware of your experience of each of them. Notice how your experience changes slightly with each sentence. In particular notice the implication of each, and how it makes you feel:

I have to buy it - I have to

I could buy it - I could

I will buy it - I will

For the vast majority of people it is possible to predict the direction or mood of the action based solely on the modal operator used. Often these work unconsciously and are rarely processed on a conscious level by your audience.

Using the Two Halves

Now that we have a perspective on the six states of Modal Operators, we can see why "You will, you will, you will" is such an unproductive approach if the audience is still at "I can't, I can't, I can't".

If we think of state 6 – I can and I will – as our desired end point, the Modal Operators in the first half (1 to 3) are very useful in establishing Rapport if we assume that a proportion of the audience are starting in one of those negative, passive or stuck states. That is where we can meet them, pick them up and lead them across the 'bridge' towards our desired endpoint.

Step One: a glimpse of what is possible or probable

First we should engage our audience. This may be your ad's headline, the title of your Presentation, the subject of an email or the strapline on the front of a brochure. In most instances this is a good opportunity to present a clear and single minded benefit and Modal Operator states 5 and 6 are good places to find them; what would this product or service enable the audience to do? And it will hook in those predisposed to your offering even if it doesn't do much for those starting in a more negative state.

However, always remember that one of the most successful and most replicated advertising headlines ever is:

Don't buy a ………. until you read this!

Step Two: accept there may be negatives

Apart from possible use in Step One, words like:

1. Can't, won't

2. Couldn't

3. Mustn't

Can be used in moderation in the opening section of your communication to establish Rapport with the audience and perhaps address the 'problem' for which we have a 'solution'.

This works particularly well with those in a negative, passive or stuck state.

I know you can't do all of this yet

Usually, just dipping back to state number 2 is enough:

A lot of people assume they might not be eligible. And I wouldn't suggest you make a decision until you have considered all the options.

Step Three: cautious use of necessity

As you build your argument and progress through the 6

Modal Operator states, you need to consider the appropriateness of using or skipping over Necessity both 3 (Negative) and 4 (Positive). Taking action because we 'have to' can be uncomfortable; so use modifying verbs in these areas with care. Behind modal operators of necessity is some undefined rule of conduct so only use them when you can be sure you will meet with acceptance of, or agreement with this rule or imperative. This is brought into the open by asking *"What would happen if you did, or did not, do this?"*

In other words imperatives that are forced or uncomfortable are counter-productive; Necessity (negative or positive) that are legitimate and appropriate can be helpful as we 'chain' into the second half of Modal Operators:

Together, we mustn't allow this awful situation to continue.

Please remember, you have to make a decision before the close-date.

Perhaps you should consider a few options.

Step Four: anything is probable

Either way, as you write your copy you can link from Steps One or Two into the other Modal Operators of the positive half (5 and 6) in a manner in which the positive orientation evolves.

Modal Operators in Probability (5) can deal with any hidden undefined rules of states 3 and 4 head on:

What if we could stop this awful situation right now?

Just imagine what would happen if you secured a place now?

That is in the form of questions; as statements they also open up the idea of action without being 'pushy' and this step is greatly helped when rapport – a meeting of minds - has been established by using Modal Operators from states 2, 3 or even 1 as described in Step Two.

What you might consider doing is ...

You may find that having a secured place is very useful.

You would then be in a very strong position.

Step Five: modal operators of possibility make things possible.

Words like 'can' and 'will' define what is considered possible. Having led your audience from a passive or 'stuck' state you are moving them gently towards the desired action. Instead of the conflict of 'Yes you can – No I can't' the systematic use of Modal Operators has brought them to a point where positive suggestions of action are appropriate and relevant.

The 'Yes you can – No I can't' situation may seem ridiculous but we frequently find marketing copy that is heavily populated with Modal Operators just from Possibility (6). (We will give you an opportunity to check this out for yourself in the following exercises.) 'You could – you can – you could – you can' is a natural result of wanting to talk about benefits and features and a reticence to address those passive or stuck states your audience may well be starting in.

So having constructed a reasonable argument you have brought your audience to a point where they are more likely to accept the state 6 closing suggestions:

If you choose to apply now.

You can do this very easily.

And you will receive a confirmation immediately.

Using Modal Operators in writing and analysing copy

Applying your understanding of Modal Operators will help the copy motivate its audience more effectively.

It won't convert everybody but it will bring along more people than not using it.

It isn't a rigid formula – use it as a guiding principle. First, you can use the six states as a way of sketching out your argument and your understanding of your audience's possible negatives by answering questions such as:

What would my audience's 'I can't' (1) or 'I couldn't' (2) be? What might the 'could' or 'would' be? (This will include the benefits)

Even if you don't use all these in your finished copy it is a useful way of structuring your ideas.

Second, you can use the sequence of the chained Modal Operators as a framework as you write your copy. Having Modal Operators is probably going to happen anyway and usually is a good thing so you might as well have a sequence and organisation that is helpful to progress your audience to the desired action.

Third, when you do have something written (either by you or someone else) and in other respects it is meeting your criteria, go through it and when you find a Modal Operator mark it 1-6.

Review the distribution. The greater the density of Modal Operators the more drive and energy the piece will have and you will need to decide what is the appropriate level and add or delete as appropriate.

Overall, you want to see a shift – sometimes referred to as a 'chain' - through the copy from the low numbered Modal Operators early-on to state 6 Possibility at the close. If your piece has a separate section that may be read as a stand-alone such as a panel, you should consider building in its own 'mini-chain' of Modal Operators.

Whilst the phasing or 'chaining' of Modal Operators needn't be followed slavishly you should avoid extreme interruptions to the flow. We have already the discussed the lack of rapport and respect that comes from piling in with lots of state 6 right from the start. Likewise, when you have artfully taken your audience from the Impossibilities they start with, through to the Probabilities of what they could do and close on the Possibilities of what they can do, are able to do and will do – you will disrupt the flow if you then use an Impossibility or Improbability at the end.

There is an old sales person's saying; when the customer says 'Yes' – stop talking!

It is amazing in the conventional construction of copy, how often a good presentation of a problem followed by a solution that the audience can agree to does not stop there. Instead it is ruined by a close that takes the audience right back to the state where they started complete with don'ts, cants and wonts.

Indeed, now that you appreciate the potential power of Modal Operators the jarring effect of such a thing will no doubt be more apparent to you.

Motivating Copy Examples

This section deals with the practicalities of using Modal Operators to motivate an audience towards taking a desired action.

Although it is not taught in this way to aspiring copywriters, it's a surprisingly easy discipline to learn and will have a significant effect on the likelihood of your copy holding an audience and shifting their attitudes and behaviour. In tests with communications that are primarily concerned with the audience taking action; Direct Response advertising and mail, the application of

Modal Operators in their optimum sequence always correlates with improvements in results.

Also, because Modal Operators are auxiliary components rather than the core content, it is easy in most instances to adjust them without interfering unduly with the main elements.

The starting point is to be able to recognise the Modal Operators that are modifying the main verbs and identify which of the six areas they belong to. This is something that becomes very easy, very quickly with a little practise. Indeed, don't be surprised if you find yourself reading through copy differently now and noting the Modal Operators (or lack of them) as you do.

Although by no means exhaustive, below is a listing of commonly used Modal Operators.

Directory of Modal Operators

1. Negative Possibility (Impossibility)

Am not

Won't

Can't

Doesn't permit

Don't choose to

Don't decide

Don't intend

Impossible

Try not

Unable to

2. Negative Probability (Improbability)

Wouldn't

Couldn't

Don't dare to

Don't deserve

Don't let

Don't prefer

Don't pretend

Don't wish

Had better not

May not

Might not

3. Negative Necessity

Mustn't

Shouldn't

Doesn't allow

Doesn't have to

It's not time

Not necessary

Ought not

Supposed not to

4. Necessity

Must

Got to

Have to

Necessary

It's time

Need to

Ought to

Should

Supposed to

5. Probability

Could

Dare to

Deserve

Had better

Let

May

Might

Prefer

Pretend

Wish

Would

6. Possibility

Can

Will

Able to

Am

Choose to

Decide

Do

Intend

It is possible

As referenced above, you may find yourself looking at all sorts of existing copy in a new light now. So let's do that as an initial exercise.

Modal Operator Exercise One

Take some pieces of marketing communication you have recently been on the receiving end of, particularly those one might assume would like to cause you to be 'motivated' in some way. Examples of direct mail are good.

1. Go through it with a pen and mark up all the Modal Operators you can find indicating which state 1 to 6 they belong to.

2. What is the distribution like? Are there a lot? Or very few?

A lot – does it seem too pushy?

A few – does it seem too inactive?

3. What is the sequence of Modal Operators?

Does it construct an argument beginning with Modal Operators from the first half; building to a close using Possibility? Does it begin with Modal Operators of Probability or Possibility? – if so does it seem assumptive? Does it include a lot of Necessity – if so does it seem bullying?

4. Overall, does it appear to have been constructed with any conscious understanding of its Modal Operators?

Yes – has this increased its ability to motivate the reader?

No – has this hindered its ability to motivate the reader?

Can you see ways in which you could adjust its use of Modal Operators to increase its ability to motivate the reader?

To dramatically change the energy and drive of copy all that is required is to: Change the frequency of Modal Operators

Higher numbers of Modal Operators make copy more energetic. Lower numbers of modified verbs make copy more matter-of-fact and impersonal.

Example: look through this piece of copy

How many Modal Operators can you find?

By sponsoring one of us older dogs for just £1 a week, you're giving us everything we need – a home, happiness and a secure future. When you sponsor us you receive news of what we've been up to, a certificate, photos and most importantly, friendship.

No, we couldn't find any either though it's a nice piece of copy for a very good cause. But could it be a little more animated? Lively? Motivating? Let's add a few modal operators.

*By sponsoring one of us older dogs for just £1 a week, you **wouldn't** just be giving us everything we need – a home, happiness and a secure future. If you **could** sponsor one of us you **would** receive news of what we've been up to, you **will** get a certificate, you **can** have photos and most importantly, you **will** have our friendship.*

Do you notice how much more energy and drive it now has? Perhaps a little too much?

If you come across text where a 'chain' of six Modal Operators from three different areas has been squeezed into 45 words of body copy you may decide it is a little excessive.

If so, you can easily adjust it back?

*By sponsoring one of us older dogs for just £1 a week, you **would** be giving us everything we need – a home, happiness and a secure future. When you sponsor us you **will** receive news of what we've been up to, a certificate, photos and most importantly, you **will** be our friend.*

You may notice how this version is more subtle and yet still has more energy and drive towards the action of becoming a sponsor than the original had.

To dramatically change the orientation of copy toward a desired action all that is required is to: Change the sequence of Modal Operators.

Example: look through this piece of copy:

Choose *to sponsor one of us older dogs for just £1 a week and you **will** be giving us everything we need – a home, happiness and a secure future. When you sponsor us you **will** receive news of what we've been up to, a certificate, photos and most importantly, your friends here **won't** forget you.*

Does the opening seem a little presumptuous and 'pushy'? Well, it does launch straight in with a Modal Operator of Possibility and follows that with two more within 35 words. And having built up a head of steam, does the ending seem rather downbeat? Well, if the reader has been engaged by the repeated Possibility the text then leaves us on a Modal Operator of Impossibility.

Example: look through this piece of copy:

*You **must** sponsor one of us older dogs for just £1 a week because you'll be giving us everything we **have to** have – a home, happiness and a secure future. You **shouldn't** forget, when you sponsor us you receive news of what we've been up to, a certificate, photos and most importantly, friendship.*

Necessity, both positive and negative, can be off-putting, seem bullying and actually be counter-productive in motivational terms.

Unless there is a genuine and acceptable imperative:

*Please remember, you **must** start sponsoring before the end of this month so that we **can** claim the extra tax relief from the government.*

Finally, before you start to analyse or change copy for yourself, consider undertaking the exercises below, which are designed to help you become more familiar with the use of Modal Operators.

Modal Operator Exercise Two

To practice inserting Modal Operators into text try this simple exercise before moving on to your own copy.

Here is a section of text intended to generate donations for a good cause:

In developing countries, the costs of surgery are far out of reach for millions of families who earn less than one pound a day - but children are saved with simple surgery in as little as 45 minutes and at a cost of as little as £150.

A donation of £15 covers the cost of sutures for one surgery...£30 covers the cost of anaesthesia...£75 helps towards training a local surgeon.

Now. Do you think you can increase its ability to carry the reader to a point where they are more likely to take action?

In the spaces between the lines, introduce words, phrases or sentences that include Modal Operators which sequence or 'chain' through to area 6. You could refer to the Modal Operator Directory.

In developing countries, the costs of surgery are far out of reach for millions of families who earn less than one pound a day – but children are saved with simple surgery in as little as 45 minutes and at a cost of as little as £150. A donation of £15 covers the cost of sutures for one surgery ...£30 covers the cost of anaesthesia...£75 helps towards training a local surgeon.

Suggestion

Here are some suggestions how that could have been done. Notice the additional drive it has in its sequence of motivation right up to the point ready for a direct request for money.

You will have your own way of doing this and that is fine – the key thing is to recognise how easy it can be to introduce the Modal Operators once you have decided on a framework of which ones you want to use in each section of the copy.

*We **wouldn't** claim to be able to help everybody. But in developing countries, even the costs of what **should** be basic surgery are far out of reach for millions of families who earn less than one pound a day - but children **could** be saved with simple surgery in as little as 45 minutes and at a cost of as little as £150. If you **could** send a donation of £15 it **would** cover the cost of sutures for one surgery...£30 **will** cover the cost of anaesthesia...£75 **can** help towards training a local surgeon.*

Modal Operator Exercise Three

This is a piece of copy intended to engage an audience about the subject of Climate Change and hopefully galvanize them into taking some action.

Look through it. Read it aloud if you can:

Climate Change

World leaders are failing to tackle global climate change. This is a major threat to all of us – but particularly to millions of people living in poverty. The situation is already critical. But disaster is just around the corner – levels of carbon dioxide, methane and nitrous oxide in the atmosphere are higher now than at any time in the last 420,000 years.

The important thing is that we all have a part to play.

There's no time to lose.

Do you think you can give it more energy and make it more motivating? Again, there are currently no Modal Operators.

Now read through this version. Again, read it aloud if you can:

Climate Change

*World leaders **can** tackle global climate change if they **choose** to. This is a major threat to all of us – but it **will** be particularly serious for millions of people living in poverty without the resources to cope. The situation is already critical and disaster **could** be just around the corner – levels of carbon dioxide, methane and nitrous oxide in the atmosphere are higher now than at any time in the last 420,000 years.*

*The good news is we **don't** have to let this happen - we*

*can't - and with your help we **won't**.*

Does it have more energy than the original? Probably yes. Is it as motivating as it could be? Well clearly there are now Modal Operators; so work through the text, identify them and mark which area 1-6 they belong to. Is there a sequence here that might be counter-productive in regards to motivating the audience?

Now, edit the text in order to change the Modal Operators in a way that will increase its motivating ability.

Climate Change

*World leaders **can** tackle global climate change if they **choose** to. This is a major threat to all of us – but it **will** be particularly serious for millions of people living in poverty without the resources to cope. The situation is already critical and disaster **could** be just around the corner – levels of carbon dioxide, methane and nitrous oxide in the atmosphere are higher now than at any time in the last 420,000 years.*

*The good news is we **don't** have to let this happen - we*

*can't - and with your help we **won't**.*

Suggestion

Here is a version of that text in which the Modal Operators 'chain' or sequence through starting from area 1 'unable' and deliver the audience up to area 6 'can' and 'will'. Read it; aloud if you can:

Climate Change

*World leaders seem **unable** to tackle global climate change. This is a major threat to all of us – but particularly to millions of people living in poverty who **don't** have the resources to cope. It **ought not** be an exaggeration to say that the situation is already critical. But disaster **could be** just around the corner – levels of carbon dioxide, methane and nitrous oxide in the atmosphere are higher now than at any time in the last 420,000 years.*

*The good news is we **can** still do something. It is possible to reverse these changes – and with your help we **will**.*

Does this use its energy more effectively to move the audience toward action?

Again, you will have your own way of achieving the result; the key is appreciating how the introduction of Modal Operators in a particular order can change copy's energy and the likelihood of it motivating action or a changed state.

Watch the Writing Copy That Motivates video at

http://www.espconsultancy.co.uk/writing_copy_that_motivates

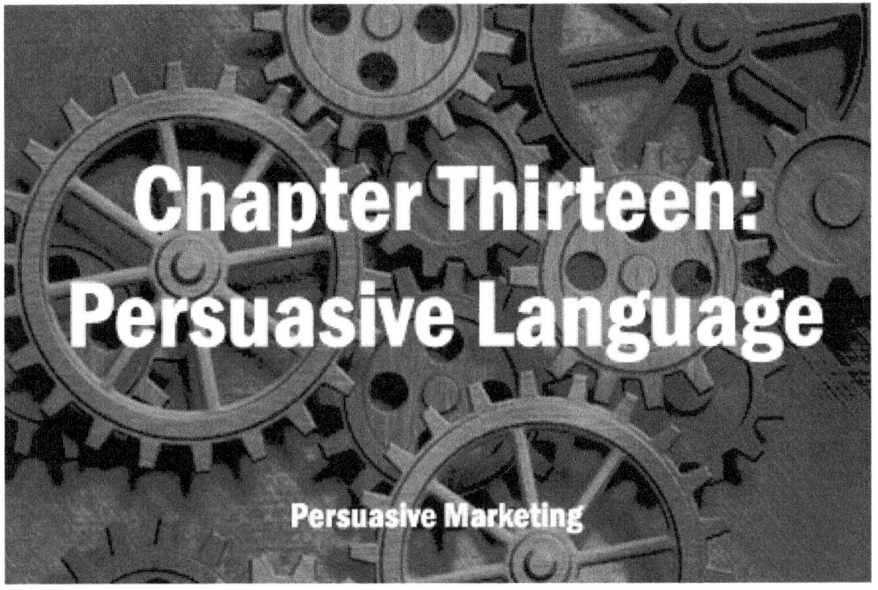

Think of the dullest, most charmless, least engaging piece of copy you have ever read or heard. It may have been a legal document or a technical specification or a directory of factual information.

Now, don't get me wrong, such documents are vital in their own context and are probably constructed that way for a purpose. But that purpose is almost certainly not engaging, persuading or motivating their audience.

Think of the most interesting, engaging and moving piece of copy you have ever read or heard. It may have been a novel, a poem, a speech or a story.

What if we could adopt just a fraction of that engagement and motivation in our own writing? Would that make our copy more effective and successful? So how do we do that? And gauge it to an appropriate level.

We could simply take elements we admire and incorporate them in our work. That's fine, but there is a danger in just borrowing things. Imagine opening up a presentation about; say, the benefits of a new office accounting system with:

I have a dream

It might just seem a bit crass or disrespectful or just inappropriate.

Or picture a headline on an advertisement for the same accounting system:

Because you're worth it

That might just look derivative and silly.

What would be much more useful is developing the understanding of where language that is more engaging and persuasive comes from and why it is more engaging and persuasive. With that understanding we can create our own copy to engage and hold more of our readers or listeners.

Whenever we have analysed copy we have always found a direct correlation between levels of success in changing the audience's beliefs or behaviour and the use of the structural techniques and language patterns in this topic.

We call them Persuasive Language to incorporate a broad mixture of language patterns that we have adapted from Neuro Linguistic Programming (NLP).

One of their common denominators is that – unlike the legal document, technical specification or directory of factual information - they are definitely not specific or precise in their language. In fact, one of the characteristics of these language patterns is that they can be ambiguous, unspecified or lacking the detail that one would need to entirely understand them. That is what engages the mind or confuses the mind or conflicts with its assumptions. The brain needs to engage in order to process these patterns and understand them – and that is what makes them 'interesting'.

After all: I have a dream

What?

An aspiration and 'goal' type dream?

Or a succession of images, thoughts, or emotions passing through the mind during sleep?

And 'have'? Have when?

Held for several years? Or experienced last night? Just thought of it now?

Of course, they could be any of these. It is ambiguous and so, loaded with meaning.

As somebody else once said; "it makes you fink dunnit?"

And: Because you're worth it

Worth what?

Worth the premium price? Worth the effort?

And if we are, the consequence 'because' - is what exactly?

Now the advertisers could simply say something like;

We put in certain ingredients and charge you extra.

However, that is both saying more but at the same time limiting itself. It begs the question 'what ingredients?' and omits any factors other than ingredients.

If they were writing one of those technical specifications they might say something like;

Our experts who are very experienced and knowledgeable put in...

propylene glycol, aloe barbadensis extract, spermaceti, trideceth-12, Chinese tea extract (camellia sinensis), cetrimonium chloride, amodimethicone, behentrimonium chloride, citric acid, chlorhexidine dihydrochloride, methylparaben, PEG-180 and hydroxyethyl cellulose

...because we really understand what makes people look and feel attractive and when we have run our exhaustive tests we have found that these formulations produce a better outcome and if you care about this as much as we do you may be prepared to seek out our products and pay an above average retail price.

Phew! Now that is very factual and precise. Perhaps too factual and precise?

And it is so long. Not something you'd want to repeat too often. In fact, it has delivered everything we might have needed but probably didn't really want to know. And raised or omitted factors we are now concerned about.

Assuming we didn't switch off just after the start. Perhaps it would have been better if we could have just made up our own meaning?

And indeed, the esteemed Martin Luther King jnr could have stood on the steps of the Lincoln Memorial on August 28, 1963 in front of 200,000 civil rights activists and announced;

Today I should like to explain to you a concept for racial equality and social justice that I have developed which encompasses specific aspects of our lives and which would change certain defined socio-economic structures of our country over the next fifty years

Thankfully he didn't. Dr King was a Baptist minister. He was a very successful orator. He knew that being factual and detailed was not always the best way to engage, excite and motivate a congregation or any sort of audience.

"I have a dream that my four little children will one day live in a nation where they will not be judged by the colour of their skin, but by the content of their character, I have a dream that one day on the red hills of Georgia the sons of former slaves and the sons of former slave owners will be able to sit down together at a table of brotherhood. I have a dream"

He also understood the value of a short, easily repeated phrase that said a lot by saying not much at all.

So what are the secrets of these engaging ambiguities? How are they made? And how can they be used by us to make our own copy more persuasive more often for more people?

The Milton Model and NLP

The founders of Neuro Linguistic Programming (NLP) Richard Bandler and John Grinder recognised in their study of communication that for the purposes of efficiency, thought is subject to an unconscious process of deletion, generalization and distortion which is influenced by pre-existing beliefs, strategies, memories, and decisions. This connected with earlier work in the 1950s by Noam Chomsky in which he developed the idea that each sentence in a language has two levels of representation — a 'deep structure' and a 'surface structure'. What is represented at the surface as spoken word or writing is a mere subset of the original thought revealing distorted assumptions, mystical thinking, over-simplification and omitted experiences.

Specifically, Bandler and Grinder studied Milton H. Erickson the eminent psychiatrist and pioneer of medical hypnosis. Broadly speaking, they identified two related types of language.

The researchers had already noted the ambiguous language commonly used by patients in their 'surface structure' when they described and talked about their issues with Dr Erickson.

What Bandler and Grinder identified were the types of questions Dr Erickson used to retrieve the information from the 'deep structure' that had been deleted, generalised and distorted to leave the ambiguities so he could reveal the underlying original thoughts, beliefs and values. They then organised these questions into a structure – The Meta Model - in a way Erickson himself had never done.

What was even more remarkable was that when they monitored and analysed Dr Erickson's ground-breaking and extremely successful Hypnotherapy sessions, they discovered that the language he instinctively used at the point where he wanted to create change also followed their Meta Model – but in reverse. They called this The Milton Model.

So The Meta Model seeks to specify distortion, deletions and generalization in a speaker's language and The Milton Model intentionally utilizes those patterns in a general, ambiguous and metaphoric way. In a clinical application such as Erickson's, this use of deliberately imprecise language to enable a person to work at an unconscious or somatic level rather than a cognitive level helped to resolve clinical issues more effectively.

However, when we adapt The Milton Model to applications in communications effectiveness – what at ESP we call Persuasive Language – we find that the patterns feature in almost all the most successful examples of communication and are a very effective aid to increase rapport, to distract the conscious mind and to access unconscious resources of your audience and lead them into an altered state.

Erickson maintained that it was not possible to consciously instruct the subconscious mind, and that authoritarian suggestions were likely to be met with resistance. The subconscious mind responds to openings, opportunities, metaphors and contradictions. Effective suggestions then should be 'artfully vague', leaving space for the subject to fill in the gaps with their own unconscious understandings.

The skilled communicator constructs these gaps of meaning in a way most suited to the audience - in a way which is most likely to produce the desired change.

I have a dream

Yes. I know just what you mean. Count me in.

Persuasive Language (The Milton Model)

As stated earlier, our analysis of advertising and marketing materials, presentations and broader communications has always found a direct correlation between levels of success in changing the audience's beliefs or behaviour and the use of these language patterns.

There is of course a fundamental advantage in being 'artfully vague'.

If you have completed the chapters on Rapport, you will recall that you are more likely to gain agreement at the abstract end of the 'hierarchy' and more likely to find disagreements as something becomes more detailed and specific. This is because the specifics will be more limiting and have a greater chance of excluding concepts from someone else's experience.

Perhaps that is why we find these patterns used extensively by top politicians.

Also, because Persuasive Language (like The Milton Model) is purposely vague and metaphoric it can be used to make indirect suggestions.

A direct suggestion merely states the goal. For example, imagine talking to someone who is extremely nervous when making a presentation:

"When you are making a presentation you will not feel nervous".

Not likely to make any changes in their state.

Whereas an indirect suggestion is less authoritative and leaves an opportunity for their own interpretation which is always going to be a better interpretation than someone else's.

For example:

"When you are making a presentation, you might find yourself feeling ever more confident".

Here, both the specific time and level of self-confidence is left unspecified.

Even more so in this example:

"When you come to a decision to make a presentation, you may find it interesting how your feelings have changed."

Here, the choice of speaking in front of the audience, the exact time, and the likely responses to the whole process are framed, but imprecise language gives the recipient the opportunity to fill in the finer details.

So, the method for increasing the effectiveness of your communications is to understand and have the ability to select and apply certain structural archetypes. Inevitably, this can be a bit 'technical' or 'heavy' at times.

So it's important to remember:

Acknowledge the jargon and the labels but be relaxed about them. The language patterns are presented in a particular order which is not necessarily their order of effectiveness for you

Having gained a fundamental appreciation of the underlying structures be flexible and experiment to measure their usefulness (or not) in what you are doing.

Adapt them to your purposes, your work, your audiences and your personal style of writing.

Most important, remember:

You almost certainly use these Persuasive Language patterns already.

They are natural parts of language.

The key is to give yourself the ability to recognise them and consciously manage your selection and usage of them when you deem it appropriate.

Once you understand the essence of what is happening in all of these examples you will be able to recognise them in your and other people's writing and be able to adjust them as you see fit.

The process of using them will soon become subconscious but reinforced by your structural understanding of (and ability to check and edit) what you are actually doing.

So bearing in mind their association with effective communications, work through this list and:

Consider how often you have come across examples of them.

Consider how often your writing includes any of these.

And consider how you might incorporate any and all of them whenever your writing needs to be more interesting and persuasive.

1. Mind Reading

Claiming to know the thoughts or feelings of another without specifying the means by which you came to have that knowledge.

"I know that you are wondering how best to apply these techniques"

"You already know, instinctively, how to do this"

2. Lost Performative

Value judgements where the performer of the value judgement is omitted.

"And it's a good thing to wonder about this sort of thing"

Who says? Well it's plausible. So why not?

3. Cause and Effect

Implying that one thing causes another, ideally linking benefits to the subject matter in order to give it credence. It doesn't need to be logically irrefutable as long as it is plausible

"As you sit there and read this, you are learning so much"

"Don't buy now, unless you want security & flexibility"

"Because you are reading this book, everything now will be so much more efficient"

Because this is ... then you'll find that ...

As you ... then you ...

4. Complex Equivalence

This is the example used at the beginning of the book. Presenting different things as equivalent or meaning the same thing. These are often similar to Cause and Effect but there's no need to get hung up on how and why – both work well.

"Developed by linguistic scientists, this approved technique is …"

"This is manufactured in Germany so reliability is guaranteed … "

5. Presuppositions

The linguistic version of assumptions.

"When you begin to use these techniques, you may discover new resources that you didn't realise you had"

"Before you agree to this, I'd like you to double check you are happy with what we've discussed"

Here, the temporal predicates "before" and "when" presuppose what the person will do and in order for them to process the following clause they must, at some level, accept that presupposition - or at least its possibility.

6. Unspecified nouns, pronouns and verbs

"People can produce great results using Persuasive Language"

Which people, specifically? (unspecified pronoun). How specifically can these people generate results? (unspecified verb). What specific results do these people generate? (unspecified noun).

"Because you're worth it"

Who is specifically? Me? Fashionable women? People In general?

Who is measuring the worth and how?

What specifically is the It that we are worth?

Being abstract means that the audience, in order to comprehend the sentence, has to make their own meaning for these unspecified elements which in the right circumstances will be much fuller and more fulfilling than any detail we could provide.

"I have a dream"

What does that actually mean? And yet how many people in that audience do you think heard that short sentence for the first time and totally related to it?

7. Lack of Referential Index

A phrase which does not define a specific part of the audience's experience. It relies on an acceptance of a generalised or abstract view.

"One can, you know"

"People do it all the time"

"Here's the thing"

Yes, I can't actually recall a specific example that I have experienced but – as long as it's plausible – it seems to be a universal truth.

8. Referential index shift

A shift in referential index occurs when the subject of the sentence shifts from one perspective to another. In the following example, first person ("I") shifts to third person ("you").

"From my perspective, I think this book has been improving your communications, your colleagues may notice that you have become more effective in your communications."

9. Comparative Deletions

Use of comparison words (e.g. more, better, best, greatest) where one or both of the objects compared is unspecified:

"The more you practice the use of this model, the better you will become at communication"

More than what? What level are we comparing it to? Better than what? Where is the benchmark?

Again, as long as it's plausible, we are tolerant of these abstractions and generalisations.

10. Universal Quantifiers

Words which generalise universally with no referential index. For example; all, every, everyone, always

"You can always improve your language skills with every conversation you have"

11. Indirect suggestion (Conversational postulates)

These are yes/no questions which are not really looking for an answer at all.

"Can you just take a moment to take a deep breath and relax?"

"Would you like a 50% buy now discount on our everyday price?"

As we process the question, we take on the suggestion.

12. Embedded questions

Directly asking questions can be intrusive, challenging and break rapport with your audience. Instead of asking the question.

"What are you thinking about?"

It can be replaced with a statement:

"I'm curious to know what you are thinking"

"I've been wondering what you are thinking for a little while now"

In the above example the question 'What are you thinking about?' is embedded in the sentence structure of a statement.

13. Embedded commands

An embedded command is typically distinguished or marked out using a subtle shift in voice tonality or gesture when speaking or a non-verbal cue in written text such as line breaks, exaggerated spacing or changes to font, colour or background.

Here we exaggerate in order to illustrate.

"You may begin to feel a sense of comfort as you begin to develop these skills in your daily life"

"Don't buy this, until you have read about this amazing discovery"

14. Tag questions

A question added after a statement in order to displace resistance and gain agreement. (Come on, we've all used this one for sure, haven't we?)

…didn't you?

…isn't it?

…have you?

…will you?

…won't you?

…haven't you?

…aren't we?

…don't you now?

…don't you think?

…and you can, can't you?

"You're coming, aren't you?"

"Do listen, will you?"

"Let's have a beer, shall we?"

"Real value for money, isn't it?"

"You're already seeing ways to use these, aren't you?"

15. Universal Yes Sets

Very useful when introducing a suggestion. Presenting statements that you know will gain agreement and doing so three times in a row establishes a pattern of acceptance in an audience.

When you then insert a suggestion the audience is more likely to agree.

The classic structure for 'yes sets' is, Universal Statement, (yes) Universal Statement (yes), Universal Statement (yes), insert suggestion.

"You are all sitting here, reading this, learning new things, and getting a great deal of value from it all."

"If you really want value for money, the best performance and great returns then act now while our limited stocks last"

16. Metaphors

Metaphors are comparisons that show how two things that are not alike in most ways are similar in one important way. An extended metaphor is a story which illustrates an important attribute of the subject.

Clearly, this can be very powerful technique in any communication as it distances the conscious mind and leads the audience into an altered state where they are more likely to take on and remember a complex message.

In advertising, there are many notable examples from the knowing use of a Bank's greenhouse that helps money grow or its pottery sheepdog that rounds up the piggy-banks through to the boy carrying home the loaf of bread through a timeline of British historical experiences.

In Therapeutic Metaphor, practitioners like Erickson used a type of conceptual metaphor presented as a story or other parallel to an entire aspect of a situation.

The purpose of this is to highlight to a person, in an effective way, some aspects and lessons that otherwise they might not be able to perceive as clearly in their current situation, or to suggest new outlooks on it.

So, consider if you have aspects of your offering that might be more effectively communicated in this form.

Conclusion

There are a few other patterns in Bandler and Grinder's Milton Model but these are the most likely to be found in our analysis of successful advertising and marketing materials.

Remember, whenever we have analysed copy we have always found a direct correlation between levels of success in changing the audience's beliefs or behaviour and the use of the Persuasive Language patterns we have adapted from The Milton Model.

And if you have been producing legal documents and technical specifications and they just seem too interesting – now you might know why.

Persuasive Language Examples

This final section deals with ways in which you can increase the persuasiveness of your copy by using adaptations of NLP's Milton Model.

Persuasive Language Exercise One

A good starting point is to assess your own use of these patterns or check out any copy that you are otherwise very familiar with.

Take a piece of writing.

Take your list of Persuasive Language.

One by one, pick a language pattern and quickly run through the copy checking for any appearances. Where you find one; mark it and code it in some way – for example notate with the appropriate 1-16 list number.

So are there any examples of 'Persuasive Language'?

Which ones?

Are they being productive in reinforcing important elements in the copy or are they being counter-productive by reinforcing insignificant points?

How frequently do they appear? Are they well distributed or crowded together?

Are some being over used?

Which ones are not being used?

If they were – how would they work?

You are the best judge of the appropriate usage. But it can be a very useful exercise to challenge your subjective judgements on appropriateness by experimenting with alternatives. Pick an example of Persuasive Language you would never normally use in a particular piece. Try it. Test it.

It might just work – or – stimulate other creative ideas.

That is one of the benefits of consciously understanding these archetypes; you can play with them, manipulate them, and easily adapt them. And see what happens.

Example: look through this piece of copy

How many Persuasive Language Patterns can you find in the segment of copy we used in the Modal Operator Exercises?

By sponsoring one of us older dogs for just £1 a week, you're giving us everything we need – a home, happiness and a secure future. When you sponsor us you receive news of what we've been up to, a certificate, photos and most importantly, friendship.

By the way, we have deliberately used the same copy example as in the earlier section. We have done this for two reasons. First, it saves us having to find a new one. Second, it demonstrates that you don't have to hand-pick a special piece of copy to illustrate these patterns – you can find them all over the place and add them to almost any copy.

Well we think there are already at least four patterns in there:

Cause and Effect (3)

Complex Equivalence (4)

Presupposition (5)

Unspecified Verb and Noun (6)

All in 45 words. So this piece of fundraising is already working hard and displaying characteristics of being 'interesting'.

By sponsoring (3) one of us older dogs for just £1 a week, you're giving (3) us everything we need – a home, happiness and a secure future (4). When you sponsor us (5) you receive news of what we've been up to (6), a certificate, photos and most importantly, friendship (6).

Persuasive Language Exercise Two

To practice inserting Persuasive Language Patterns into text try this simple exercise before moving on to your own copy.

Again, we have deliberately used a copy example also used in the section on Modal Operators because you don't have to hand-pick a special piece of copy to show how easy it is to add these patterns.

In developing countries, the costs of surgery are far out of reach for millions of families who earn less than one pound a day - but children are saved with simple surgery in as little as 45 minutes and at a cost of as little as £150.

A donation of £15 covers the cost of sutures for one surgery...£30 covers the cost of anaesthesia...£75 helps towards training a local surgeon.

Might I suggest that you take the copy above and adapt, rewrite or whatever it takes for you to experiment with some Persuasive Language patterns. Here are some suggestions, *with the pattern highlighted in italics*, to show how these patterns can be usefully applied.

Suggestions

Here are our suggestions – yours are probably better

1. Mind Reading

I'm sure you're aware that in developing countries, the costs of surgery are far out of reach for millions of families who earn less than one pound a day - but children are saved with simple surgery in as little as 45 minutes and at a cost of as little as £150.

2. Lost Performative

In developing countries, the costs of surgery are far out of reach for millions of families who earn less than one pound a day. *It's dreadful to think that children are dying who could be* saved with simple surgery in as little as 45 minutes and at a cost of as little as £150.

3. Cause and Effect

In developing countries, the costs of surgery are far out of reach for millions of families who earn less than one pound a day - but children are saved with simple surgery in as little as 45 minutes and at a cost of as little as £150.

A donation of £15 *means that* sutures can be bought for one surgery …£30 *means that* anaesthesia can be paid for …£75 *means that* a local surgeon can be trained.

4. Complex Equivalence

In developing countries, *the costs of surgery are far out of reach* for millions of families who earn less than one pound a day *and children die* who could have been saved with simple surgery in as little as 45 minutes and at a cost of as little as £150.

5. Presuppositions

Your donation of £15 will cover the cost of sutures for one surgery...*a gift* of £30 covers the cost of anaesthesia...and £75 *from you* will help towards training a local surgeon.

6. Unspecified Nouns & Verbs

In *developing countries*, the costs of *surgery* are far out of reach for millions of *families* who earn less than one pound a day - but *children* are *saved* with simple *surgery* in as little as 45 minutes and at a cost of as little as £150.

But together *we* can *change* this. A donation of £15 *covers* the cost of sutures for one *surgery*... £30 *covers* the cost of anaesthesia ...£75 *helps* towards *training* a local surgeon.

7. Lack of Referential Index

In developing countries, the costs of surgery are far out of reach for millions of families who earn less than one pound a day – *that's the way it is.*

But children can be saved with simple surgery in as little as 45 minutes and at a cost of as little as £150. *It happens all the time in our own hospitals.*

8. Referential Index Shift

In developing countries, the costs of surgery are far out of reach for millions of families who earn less than one pound a day. *We* know that children's lives can be saved with simple surgery in as little as 45 minutes and at a cost of as little as £150 and *your* donation of £15 will cover the cost of sutures for one surgery...£30 will cover the cost of anaesthesia...£75 will help towards training a local surgeon.

9. Comparative Deletions

In developing countries conditions are *worse* than ever and the costs of surgery are now out of reach for millions of families who earn less than one pound a day. But we can make it *better* - children can be saved with simple surgery in as little as 45 minutes and at a cost of as little as £150.

10. Universal Quantifiers

Everyone appreciates that in developing countries; the costs of surgery are far out of reach for millions of families who earn less than one pound a day.

But *we can always* make a difference when we want to - especially when children can be saved with simple surgery in as little as 45 minutes and at a cost of as little as £150.

11. Indirect Suggestion

In developing countries, the costs of surgery are far out of reach for millions of families who earn less than one pound a day – where children die who could have been saved with simple surgery in as little as 45 minutes and at a cost of as little as £150.

Can you imagine saving those children with a simple donation of £15 covering the cost of sutures for one surgery...£30 covering the cost of anaesthesia...£75 helping towards training a local surgeon.

12. Embedded Questions

When we think about developing countries, where the costs of surgery are far out of reach for millions of families who earn less than one pound a day and many children die who could have been saved with simple surgery in as little as 45 minutes and at a cost of as little as £150.

It's natural for us to ask ourselves *what are you prepared to do about this?* When a donation of just £15 covers the cost of sutures for one surgery...£30 covers the cost of anaesthesia...£75 helps towards training a local surgeon.

13. Embedded Commands

In developing countries, the costs of surgery are far out of reach for millions of families who earn less than one pound a day - but simple surgery in as little as 45 minutes and at a cost of as little as £150 will *save children's lives when you give a donation* of £15 you will cover the cost of sutures for one surgery...£30 covers the cost of anaesthesia...£75 helps towards training a local surgeon.

14. Tag Questions

In developing countries, the costs of surgery are far out of reach for millions of families who earn less than one pound a day – and many children die. *It is a disgrace isn't it?*

Especially when children can be saved with simple surgery in as little as 45 minutes and at a cost of as little as £150 *don't you think?*

15. Universal Yes Sets

We all understand that life is tough in developing countries. And that the *costs of surgery are far out of reach for millions of families who earn less than one pound a day.*

We all know that lots of children die unnecessarily. And now we can save many of those children with a small donation.

16. Metaphors

... and the kind stranger travelled across the land where so many of the children were sick and dying. And wherever he went, he would sit with a sick child; sometimes for an hour sometimes for only half an hour and when he did the child would awake and smile at his parents and be well again. And the stranger would sit with another child, and another – but there were always too many children for him to help and the people said 'if only someone could help him' ...

As I said, yours are probably much better. But either way, these patterns do add interest to copy and offer the opportunity to engage and stimulate the thought processes of your audience members.

Again, you will have your own way of achieving the best results for you; the key is appreciating how these Persuasive Language patterns are constructed and practising ways to introduce them appropriately into your copy.

They are fundamental to the way most of us express ourselves so they will appear anyway.

Use the lists provided to help you spot them, appreciate them and consciously decide the appropriateness and usefulness of adding or omitting them.

Watch the Persuasive Language video at

http://www.espconsultancy.co.uk/persuasive_language

---0---

Now you have everything you need to create your own original, unique, measurable, Persuasive Marketing. So, in the words of a world famous brand all that is left is to 'Just do it!'

Good luck.

About the Authors – Jim Brackin

As a Creative Director Jim was a committee member of the Direct Marketing Association (DMA), the Creative Council (Chairman 1995-97) and a member of the DMA Awards Committee, Fellow of the IDM, a regular awards judge and winner of over 60 awards for creativity, strategy and effectiveness.

Now a student of applied psychology Jim is a qualified Hypnotherapist, a Master Practitioner of Neuro-linguistics and a Master Practitioner of Time Line Therapy.

Jim has been the body language expert for Sky News, interviewed on BBC radio and published in Cosmopolitan, Woman's Own and The Daily Mirror.

About the Authors – Glyn Parry

Glyn Parry's career includes senior agency and client-side experience. At Ogilvy & Mather Direct in London that he worked on a number of successful and award winning direct marketing campaigns for major brands including Ford and Save the Children. As Advertising and Direct Marketing Manager at Xerox, Glyn was responsible for TV and press advertising but was also instrumental in developing the company's use of database marketing and telemarketing.

Having been on both sides of the (sometimes traumatic) process involved in briefing, planning, developing and signing-off campaigns, Glyn was fascinated by how psychology and advertising interact and began to also train in clinical applications.

Glyn is a qualified Hypnotherapist, a Master Practitioner of Neuro Linguistic Programming and a Master Practitioner of Time Line Therapy.

Persuasive Marketing

The use of NLP in Marketing & Advertising

www.espconsultancy.co.uk

© James Brackin & Glyn Parry 2013